Cambrian Rail

Album

Cambrian Railways
Album

C.C.Green MBE

LONDON

IAN ALLAN LTD

CYFLWYNIAD

I wyr Rheilffordd y Cambrian a fu'n fodd i greu atgofion am wyliau hapus i filoedd a oeddynt yn blant yr adeg honno; ac i'r bobol garedig hynny a'm croesawodd ar eu haelwydydd ac a roes imi fenthyg darliniau ac adrodd wrythyf bopeth a allent ei gofio am yr hen Cambrian.

DEDICATION

To the men who made the Cambrian Railways work and who made possible the happy holiday memories of thousands who were children then; and to the kindly people who made me welcome at their firesides, lent me their pictures, and told me all they could remember about the old Cambrian.

First published 1977

ISBN 0 7110 0784 5

Published by Ian Allan Ltd, Shepperton, Surrey,
and printed in the United Kingdom by
Ian Allan Printing Ltd.

Contents

Left: One of a batch of four 4-4-0 type express engines built by Sharp Stewart in 1895. No 84 was renumbered No 1107 by the GWR when the Cambrian was absorbed in 1922. A sister engine No 82 was smashed in the tragic head-on collision at Abermule on 26 January 1921./*From a painting by George F. Heiron*

Acknowledgements

Photographs have been credited as far back as possible to the photographer where known, or to the organisation which commissioned them or to the donor. Besides these, much help in conversation and correspondence was given by:

J. E. Benbow, R. Bennett, Birmingham Central Library, J. I. C. Boyd, H. W. Burman, John Burman, W. A. Camwell, G. H. W. Clifford, C. R. Clinker, Lord Davies, J. E. Davies, J. Elwyn Davies, J. S. Davies, W. J. K. Davies, D. H. Davis, George Dow, Dyfed (Aberystwyth) County Library, W. H. A. Edwards, F. W. Evans, W. Evans, T. H. Fenn, A. E. S. Fluck, W. R. Fryer, P. J. Garland, G.E.C.-Marconi Electronics Ltd., L. T. George, A. M. Gunn, Lewis Hamer, E. W. Hannen, H. Harris, W. E. Hayward, F. E. Hemming, S. H. P. Higgins, Dr. J. R. Hollick, Evan Howells, J. Hughes, S. Humphries, W. Humphries, Hunslet Engine Co, Ltd., Elfyn Jenkins, Isaac and Arthur Jenkins, Ben Jones, D. Jones, Elwyn V. Jones, J. Jordan, J. M. Lloyd, O. Lloyd, Lord Londonderry, R. W. Miller, Dick Mills, E. R. Mountford, The North British Locomotive Co. Ltd., Miss A. Owen, David Owen, Mrs. E. Owen, E. W. Owen, G. Owen, Mrs Nansi Owen, G. Archer Parfitt, R. Y. Pickering & Co. Ltd., G. H. Platt, Albert Potts, Lord Powis, Powys Area Library, The Powysland Museum, John Rees, Harry Rees, J. P. Richards, John D. Rogers, Ralph T. Russell, Salop County Library, T. Shuttleworth, Mrs Spoonley, Robert

Stephensons & Hawthorns, D. H. Stuart, E. E. Thomas, Thomas Wynne Thomas, O. Veltom, G. Venables, Vulcan Foundry Ltd., L. Ward, G. Weaver, P. B. Whitehouse, G. Dudley Whitworth, E. H. Williams, J. Williams, J. Williamson, Col. Sir Owen W. Williams-Wynn C.B.E., G. E. Barrett, H. Morgan.

In particular, my especial thanks to three gentlemen – Ifor Higgon, Mike Morton Lloyd and the late Eric Thomas, who have so generously shared with me the results of their own research; to many officials and departments of British Rail; and to the Librarian, Keeper of Prints and staff of the National Library of Wales, for a great deal of assistance in many ways. For reading the proofs I am most grateful to Messrs. P. J. Garland and W. F. B. Price.

Introduction

A railway consists of many more things besides engines and trains. People and products and their traffic requirements called the trains into being, the loads and the countryside dictated the engine design and many supporting services had to be established before a single train could be run. The money available dictated how good the engines and trains could be and how well they and the track could be maintained; and Parliament, by Board of Trade Regulation, dictated the minimum standards required for safety, wherein so many companies were apt to fall short to preserve their profits.

Of all railways the Cambrian epitomised the struggle against all odds to adjust to the stresses imposed upon it by circumstance and to maintain itself as a going concern. Even at its best it was a total failure in producing monetary wealth for its shareholders. Its greatest riches lay in its fund of friendship, goodwill and service towards the countryside for which it carried and towards the holidaymakers it conducted to the coast. It had no great or famous locomotive prototypes which set trends in design, not did it have any ugly ones; the general run of them left an impression of workmanlike neatness and the stock list exemplified admirably the sound products of the leading private makers. By the practice of absorbing minor unprofitable branch systems, coupled with occasional shopping expeditions into the second-hand market, the Cambrian added to its own locomotive stock a collection of the most delightful examples of small tank engines to be owned by any one company.

There was besides a touch of timelessness about the Cambrian. It seemed to come from a saner world than our own. Its devotees forgave it its small irregularities, its impromptu halts at nowhere and its longer halts in the passing loops, where those going on holiday could gaze across with smug superiority at the homegoers looking with envious eyes from the other halted train.

Among those countless holidaymakers it carried would be fishermen seeking peace by the beautiful rock-studded streams crossed and re-crossed many times by the line itself, walkers heading for the mountains and above all the children. To their ears the roar of braking on wheels as the coastwards train burst out of Talerddig cutting was music – an overture, perhaps, to the steady quadruple drum-beats of the bogie coaches racing down the Dovey Valley and ringing out loud and clear 'Down-to-the-beach, down-to-the-beach, down-to-the-beach'. The six-wheelers, of course, rolled out a dignified 'Soon-we'll-be, On-the-beach, Soon-we'll-be, On-the-beach . . .''

It was a long journey in terms of time but well worth enduring, for at the end lay the sea, the beach, the rocks and pools – and a high tea served by one of that great legion of landladies named Mrs Davies, Mrs Evans, Mrs Jenkins, Mrs Jones, Mrs Parry or Mrs Thomas and not forgetting Mrs Meredith, Mrs Morgan, Mrs Owen, Mrs Richards, or Mrs Lewis or Mrs Rees.

Author's note

In the 1890s a number of place-names were roughly anglicised to assist the visitors. This process has been reversed in later years and in the text the spelling and naming used is that found to be current when the photograph was taken. Also, the Cambrian had no consistent policy for commissioning official photographs. Anything we have is by pure happenstance, both in existence and in quality.

The Railways of North & Central Wales

The map shows how the rival companies had the Cambrian completely surrounded and cut off from all hopes of any lucrative through traffic. It is intended to be diagrammatic only, particularly as to the precise routes taken by the other companies. The dots represent the approximate positions of stations to convey some idea of the relative density of their local facilities. All is generally as pre-1922.

The minor branch known as the Trefonen or the Treflach went to Coed y Go and was built privately by Thomas Savin to serve his coal and brick interests. There was also a tramway from Coed y Go to the canal at Redruth. The Crickheath and other early tramways around Llanymynech and Pant, too, have had to be left off, because their tiny lengths would have confused the main presentation.

Dovey Junction, opened as Glandyfi, later became Glandovey Junction. Llanfihangel is now Llandrc. Barmouth Junction only a few years ago woke up to find it had become Morfa Mawddach. Ballast Hole, Borth, and another Ballast Hole north of Tonfanau were once extra staff stations. Garth, between Arthog and Penmaenpool, was a busy little mineral siding like so many others now long

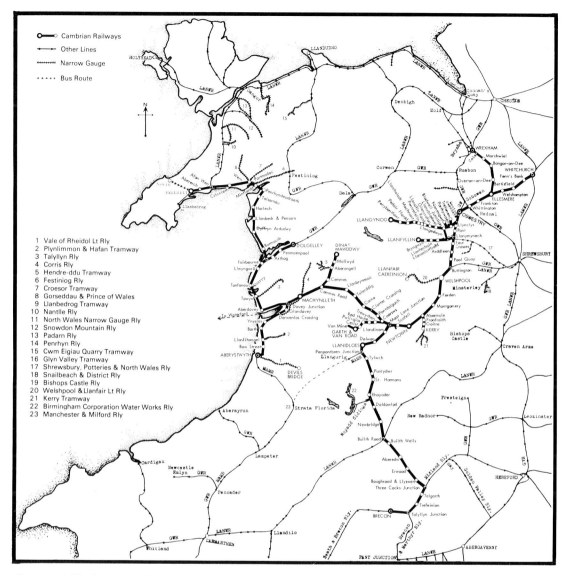

Cambrian Railways
Other Lines
Narrow Gauge
Bus Route

1 Vale of Rheidol Lt Rly
2 Plynlimmon & Hafan Tramway
3 Talyllyn Rly
4 Corris Rly
5 Hendre-ddu Tramway
6 Festiniog Rly
7 Croesor Tramway
8 Gorseddau & Prince of Wales
9 Llanbedrog Tramway
10 Nantlle Rly
11 North Wales Narrow Gauge Rly
12 Snowdon Mountain Rly
13 Padarn Rly
14 Penrhyn Rly
15 Cwm Eigiau Quarry Tramway
16 Glyn Valley Tramway
17 Shrewsbury, Potteries & North Wales Rly
18 Snailbeach & District Rly
19 Bishops Castle Rly
20 Welshpool & Llanfair Lt Rly
21 Kerry Tramway
22 Birmingham Corporation Water Works Rly
23 Manchester & Milford Rly

disappeared. The forerunner of Fairbourne, before
Barmouth Bridge was opened, was aptly named Barmouth
Ferry and Fairbourne itself was by local request to have been
Ynysfaig. It had been built by the McDougal Estate, which
had bought all the surrounding land for development under
the name of Fairbourne, and the Cambrian was given the
option of buying the station off the developers within five
years if it proved profitable. 'Unfortunately', the locals were
told, 'the nameboards have already been painted'!
Unfortunately, too, it has not been possible to fit in the
Soloman Andrews Tramway, of which parts became the
basis of the Fairbourne Miniature Railway.
    Caia by Wrexham, Wern west of Portmadoc, and Weston
Wharf south of Oswestry were the Cambrian's three goods-
only stations. Two minor branches, Sweeney by Weston and

Tonfanau Quarry, were only just long enough to merit the
name and Cambrian engines had to proceed well off the main
to work them. Besides these there were a number of sidings
for special traffic, but arrangements could be made for
ordinary goods at some of them.
    All the terminal branches had gone out of business
through lack of traffic before the Beeching closures of 18
January, 1965; and after this date only Buttington to
Aberystwyth and Dovey Junction to Pwllheli remained in
regular service. Of the inland stations only Welshpool,
Newtown, Caersws and Machynlleth have remained open,
with Borth and Aberystwyth to represent the original four
'little lines', one can still wait for one's connection at Dyfi
Junction. The coast has fared better, as only Afon Wen has
been lost.

7

From the beginning to 1857

In the beginning there were the central lands of Wales – the heartlands, as Professor Bowen has called them – with a few fertile valleys, many narrow and steep-sided ones, and many more square miles of infertile mountains. Beyond the mountains the coastal pockets were separated from one another by cliff and rock.

The people were hard-working and frugal and livings were not easily got, except on the richer soils of the wide valleys. These were held mainly by a squirearchy much given to absenteeism, which was often reflected in the run-down condition of their estates. The industrial revolution had not touched them nor would it ever alter their lives directly.

The main sources of energy were the muscles of men and horses, as few estates by then had steam engines; these and water power were more likely to be found in mines and mills. The rounded haycocks were pitched up by hand and threshing was done by hand-flail. The hilly areas supported large flocks of the small native sheep, which can prosper there having twice as many mouths to pick out the thin grasses and twice as many legs to propel the searchers per hundredweight of mutton and wool as their much larger, softer English cousins. Cattle, the ancestors of the Welsh Blacks, were numerous along all the valleys, and most households had their own milch cows.

Because of the seasonal nature of the farming and the need to find work all the year round, the hill folk combined agriculture with the search for minerals and many were both labourer and farmer besides being miners or quarry men.

Manufacture was still not prolific, being mainly production of Welsh flannel, the descendant of the home-spun 'frise of Cambria' of mediaeval times. Much of this went away by waggons along the Severn Valley or by the Montgomeryshire and Shropshire Union canal systems after it had been woven in the steam-powered mills of Newtown, which had become the main manufacturing centre.

The road system was simple, a skein of narrow ways following the valleys and connected by occasional pass-roads crossing the watersheds. Often these last were the old green ways of pedlar and pack-horse, such as Ffordd Gam Elen which is now, as it was then, a remote passage-way across the high Berwyns. The scanty coach services along these roads were adequate for the demand, as only the wealthy and the merchants could afford comfort when travelling and the rest rode in carts or on horseback – or went on foot.

Transport over the sloping fields was often by 'car llusg' – a practical and ingenious arrangement, half travois and half sledge. Because of its stable attachment to the horse's harness via wooden shafts, it avoided the dangers of over-running inherent in the man-guided sledges of the slate quarries; with them it needed only a moment's inattention for the sledge-hand to be crippled under a quarter of a ton of careering slates.

By the toiling standards of the time the area had considerable mineral wealth. In the main it left the mines by sledge and pack-horse or cart, usually in the direction of the coast, where many small sloops and brigs plied out of vestigial harbours or from as high up the estuaries of the Dyfi and of the Dysynni as they could be floated.

Traffic down the Dwyryd and the Glaslyn had ceased already with Maddock's reclamation of the

estuary by the construction of the Cob, along which ran the gravity- and horse-operated Festiniog Railway. This innovation, the 1ft 11½in. gauge brainchild of C. E. Spooner, which connected the quarries of Festiniog with the still new harbour of Portmadoc, was only a foretaste of how the new form of transport could, overnight, ruin the old and yet provide more work in other ways.

Promoters, politicians and people argued, wrangled and often indulged in bitter invective against one another for years before any part of a railway got built. The records of the proceedings before the formation of the four little companies which were to become the Cambrian provide wonderful examples of the eloquence, the wit in debate and the brilliant liveliness – 'hwyl' – in which the people of Wales excel.

Railway companies needed individual Acts of Parliament before they could become lawful bodies with powers to buy land and build and run their lines. When their Bills were presented to Parliament by a local supporting Member they could be opposed by other Members supposedly on abstract grounds of what was best for the countryside. In fact the opposition was usually inspired by rival companies wishing to build an alternative and to secure for it the traffic expected: or wishing to prevent the formation of the proposed company because it might lessen their profits by draining off some of their traffic to perhaps a better route. So from 1836 onwards there flourished a solemn array of proposal and counter-proposal of survey and alternative route, with all the attendant legal and political machinations. Until 1853 this produced nothing other than meaningless prospectuses and the expense accounts of the professionals involved. Even then so little progress followed that the Rev. Samuel Roberts wrote a doleful letter to the Shrewsbury Chronicle to the effect that 'it was 1854 and never yet have we had the pleasure of a trip on a Montgomeryshire railway'. This was the true spirit in which the Cambrian lines were eventually conceived: it was not that they were needed and had great commercial futures, merely that the local people felt they were missing out by not having any railways.

By 1853, when the promoters of the Llanidloes & Newtown Railway got their enabling Act, the opportunity for any centrally situated railway to become a link in an important transport route had been argued away for all time. A potentially fast route for the Irish Mail via the valleys of the Severn and the Dovey or the Mawddach had been bypassed by the London & North Western's North Coast route to Holyhead on the Island of Anglesey; and the great way between Manchester and the North and the potentially great port of Milford Haven had been provided by the Great Western's taking over the Shrewsbury & Chester interests and linking with its South Wales lines via joint lines shared with the North Western. Thus two great companies separately pursued policies of watching and listening to accounts of the affairs of the little companies, of obtaining representation on the tentative boards of directors (openly or otherwise), of supporting to weaken the other's cause, and of withdrawing support when one of the little companies looked like gaining strength in its own right, all paid off. The local promoters were left with nothing but their own internal traffic and no choice other than which of the many alternative, difficult valleys the lines should take. Right from the start, the little companies had to face the situations which dogged the lines all their days and gave rise to the affectionately bestowed cognomen *'yr hen Gambrian druan'* – the poor old Cambrian.

As already mentioned, the Llanidloes & Newtown Railway was the first to get its powers. These enabled it to build a railway which had no connection with any other. Its powers to extend later to Oswestry were defeated by 1855, when the Oswestry & Newtown Railway bill received

assent. And so it went on. The Newtown & Machynlleth Railway powers followed in 1857 and those of the Oswestry, Ellesmere & Whitchurch Railway in 1861, each line competing with its neighbour for subscribers, labour and materials.

A fifth candidate for the combination which would eventually become the Cambrian was the Aberystwith & Welsh Coast Railway, authorised in stages from 1861 until it too joined in 1865. The Mid Wales Railway was authorised earlier in 1859, but 'enjoyed' an uneasy separate existence in near-bankruptcy until the Cambrian started to work it in 1888. Other separate promotions were the Mawddwy Railway in 1865, which was operated by the Cambrian from 1911, and the Van Railway in 1873, which was operated by the Cambrian from 1896.

Directly fostered promotions which the Cambrian worked virtually from their opening were the Wrexham & Ellesmere Railway, authorised in 1885 and worked first in 1895; the Tanat Valley Light Railway, authorised in 1899 and worked from 1904; and the 2ft 6in-gauge Welshpool & Llanfair Light Railway, authorised in 1899 and worked from 1903.

The last fling in extension of the Cambrian domain was the acquisition of the 1ft $11\frac{1}{2}$in-gauge Vale of Rheidol Light Railway, authorised in 1897, opened in 1902 and taken over in 1913. It was this minor addition which was to bring the Cambrian the unique distinction of owning the only surviving pre-grouping line in the British Rail system still using steam as its only service motive power.

1857 – 1864: and a little way beyond

Then came the contractors and their engines; and the first and greatest contractor was David Davies of Llandinam. Such was the haste of the people of Llanidloes to have their railway that the plans, sections and specifications of the two miles to Morfodion were to be inspected at 11 o'clock on 2 October 1855, the tenders were to be in by 7 o'clock the same evening and the ceremony of cutting the first sod was to be held the next day. The local man knew his ground and undercut two rivals of considerable standing. Mr Whalley cut the first sod instead of Mrs Ann Owen, who took offence because she had not been asked before the publication of a notice which said she would be so doing.

The construction advanced well, and David Davies was awarded the contracts for the rest of the Llanidloes & Newtown Railway. He built from Llanidloes to Llandinam using only men and horses, and carted all imported materials from the canal terminal at Newtown. Then in 1857 he leased the line from the company and *Dove*, the first locomotive, was dragged on 'timber carriages' over the rough roads from Oswestry. The motive power was fourteen horses, and three more engines and some rolling stock followed by the same means. True always to his strong religious principles, when one of the cortèges failed to complete its journey by Saturday night it stood in Newtown High Street until the following Monday. The line was opened formally on 2 September 1859 and was operated by David Davies.

During this period, David Davies took Thomas Savin into partnership. Comparing the value to the railways they built of these two men, it was the dogged reliability of David Davies which saved the Llanidloes & Newtown and soon after the Newtown and Machynlleth, and the brasher enthusiasm and flair of Thomas Savin which enabled the building of the Oswestry & Newtown and of the Oswestry, Ellesmere & Whitchurch. The partnership was short-lived; it was dissolved from 29 October 1860 and the two men went their separate ways. Savin was in and out of partnership with others until his bankruptcy on 5 February 1866. Much of his deficiency was represented by already worthless shares in the companies whose lines he had built, which were all he could set against his debts to manufacturers from whom he had ordered locomotives and rolling stock in his own name. Even land stood in the names of 'Mr Savin and his Inspectors'. His reckless driving on with the Aberystwith & Welsh Coast route before negotiations with landowners were completed, brought lawsuits and compensation payments galore. By such intermingling of his own finances with those of the companies, he assumed the right to use engines wherever he wished regardless of the location of the nominal owning company. Small wonder, then, that an earlier writer should assume that a list of engines he found was the Cambrian stock list; in fact, it was either Savin's own list of the engines he was using or at best a first offer to the Cambrian when his complex affairs were being unravelled.

Another partnership, Watson and Overend, took on the job of completing the Mid-Wales Railway, the second of the early 'outsiders' which would eventually join the Cambrian. They also made the mistake of accepting shares and securities as payment for their work, but otherwise the Mid Wales, too, could never have been built.

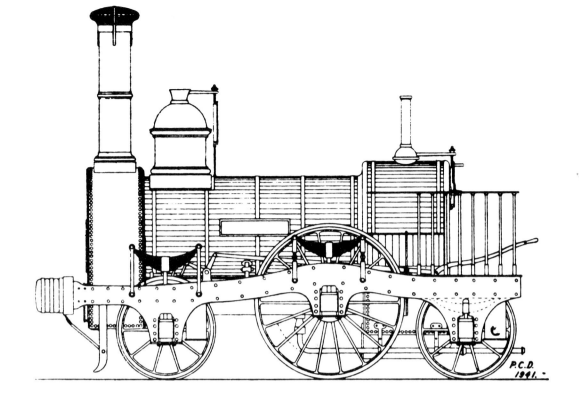

Top left: David Davies. The able and forthright teetotal Calvinist Methodist 'top sawyer'. He ventured first into construction, then, as 'Davies the Ocean', he became one of the great coal-owners. He professed to be a graduate in the 'University of Observation'. *National Library of Wales.*

Above: Dove, Sharps No.55 of October 1839, ran originally on the Birmingham & Derby Junction Railway for whom she made trouble by being 'out of gauge' when run on London & Birmingham rails. She did little better for David Davies and her working pressure of only 55 lb per square inch made her a doubtful buy. *The Locomotive Magazine.*

Right: Thomas Savin. The 'small haberdasher' who rose to be a 'railway king', then fell into bankruptcy, all within ten years. His mistaken way to power was to accept too many shares in lieu of payment for work on lines which could never pay. Without such an idealistic contractor few of the lines which became the Cambrian would ever have been built. *Top Sawyer.*

Above: The Sharp Stewart saddle-tank *Milford* was bought by David Davies to complete the Llanidloes & Newtown and arrived by horse traction to be isolated around March 1859. Originally she had no cab and water was fed into her boiler by a steam donkey-pump. Probably she was sold to the Cambrian when David Davies went on to coal mining. *Collection C. C. Green.*

Below: The first locomotive venture of the Lilleshall Iron Company bore their Works No.1, and appeared in the London Exhibition of 1862. Savin bought her in December 1863. She became Cambrian No.21, Ballast Tank Engine, and was sold in 1868. *The Locomotive Magazine.*

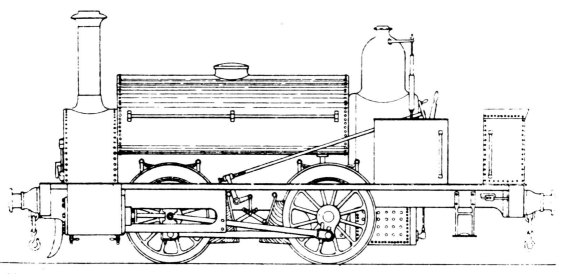

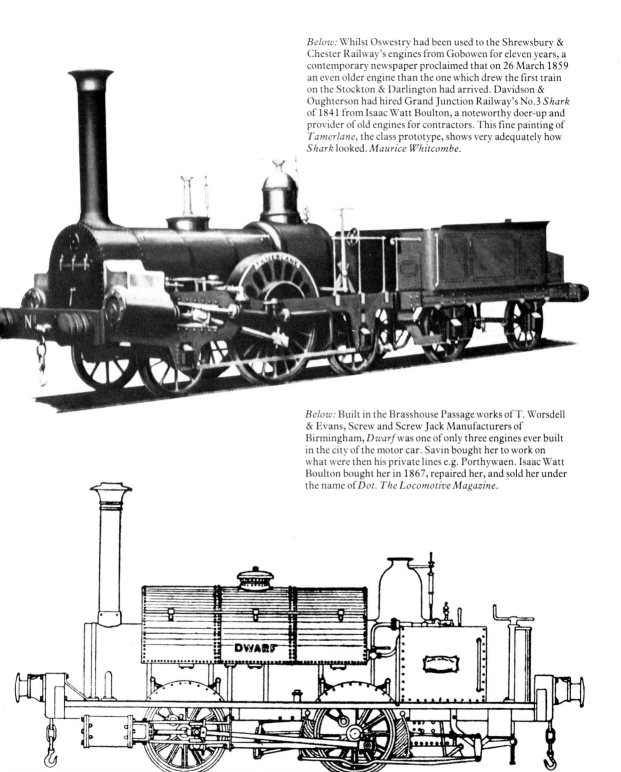

Below: Whilst Oswestry had been used to the Shrewsbury & Chester Railway's engines from Gobowen for eleven years, a contemporary newspaper proclaimed that on 26 March 1859 an even older engine than the one which drew the first train on the Stockton & Darlington had arrived. Davidson & Oughterson had hired Grand Junction Railway's No.3 *Shark* of 1841 from Isaac Watt Boulton, a noteworthy doer-up and provider of old engines for contractors. This fine painting of *Tamerlane*, the class prototype, shows very adequately how *Shark* looked. *Maurice Whitcombe.*

Below: Built in the Brasshouse Passage works of T. Worsdell & Evans, Screw and Screw Jack Manufacturers of Birmingham, *Dwarf* was one of only three engines ever built in the city of the motor car. Savin bought her to work on what were then his private lines e.g. Porthywaen. Isaac Watt Boulton bought her in 1867, repaired her, and sold her under the name of *Dot. The Locomotive Magazine.*

15

Above: Safe ashore after her tow across the Dovey in a barge from Ynyslas, behind the steamer *James Conley*, Thomas Savin's *Merion* poses with her footplate crew on Aberdovey quay as the fist engine to get there. With Cardigan she ran the train services north until the line from Dovey Junction was completed. The Class 1 Manning Wardle saddle-tank featured prominently in the construction of the lines which became the Cambrian and six passed into Cambrian stock after the sort-out of Thomas Savin's bankruptcy. *Enterprise* (known as the 'Black Donkey,) became Cambrian No.1 and had been hauled by road (as were *Dove*, *Squirrel* and *Milford*) to work on the isolated Llanidloes & Newtown. David Davies bought *Llandinam* in 1861 for his work on the Newtown and Machynlleth. Savin bought another eight, of which five (including one bought from Brecon & Merthyr funds), became Cambrian Nos. 13 *Whixhall*, (re-named Green Dragon) 14 *Nantclwyd*, 17 *Merion*, 18 *Cardigan* and 24 *Borth*. *Pioneer* and *Hereford* became Brecon & Merthyr's *Blanche* and *Lady Cornelia* respectively, and *Usk* kept her own name until the Brecon & Merthyr acquired a second Usk, after which the older engine got dubbed *Little Usk*. The Cambrian classed their six as 'Ballast Tank Engines' until this work was belatedly completed. All were sold by 1875.

There was also a four-wheeled Class 4 Manning Wardle tank called *Tiny*. Ordered for the Hereford, Hay & Brecon, *Tiny* was 'diverted' into the Cambrian area and worked Savin's own coal trains.

Besides hiring of engines for constructional work and short-term chartering of steamers, such as the *James Conley*, a passenger-carrying paddle steamer named the *Elizabeth* was chartered for a much longer term. This was used to ferry passengers from trains propelled down the curving bank from Ynyslas to a quay on the east bank of the Leri. The shunt and the crossing to Aberdovey took only 33 min, a time which was never equalled by the replacement rail connection along the north shore of the Dovey Estuary. When the new all-rail connection from Machynlleth was completed it became known as 'The Doveyation'. *J. Parry.*

Above right: No. 16 in the 'mystery' list, this Manning Wardle 0-6-0 of 1862 went into Brecon & Merthyr stock as that company's No.6. She was named after the Brecon & Merthyr's Chairman, John Parry de Winton. The Cambrian ordered six similar engines in 1866, but could not afford them, so the makers sold them, four to the Taff Vale and two to the London Brighton & South Coast. Another Manning Wardle tender engine, an 0-4-0, became Cambrian No 2. At least eight more engines have been traced as having worked for the contractors. *National Library of Wales.*

Right: In 1863 the *Illustrated London News* marked the completion of the third of the little lines with this engraving. The temporary nature of the station is evident, but under construction beyond it is the engine shed which lasted to the end of steam. *Illustrated London News.*

The look of the early railways

The character and appearance of each of the little railways form a delightful and interesting collection of diversities. Their backgrounds were some of the loveliest countryside that one could possibly wish to see. The 'stage props' – cuttings, embankments, abutments and bridges – were planned by Benjamin Piercy with considerable forethought to use as much local material as possible – as little as possible was to be brought in at greater cost. Stations and other buildings followed suit, but often were not completed until the line had been running for a year or two – or even longer.

Top right: Dolwen, a typical single-storey station of the Llanidloes & Newtown. It was run by one of the Cambrian's very few station mistresses, Miss Anne Jenkins. As a little girl six years old she would have seen the arrival of the great modern invention – the railway train – and she lived right through its best years until 1936. *C. C. Green.*

Below: The bridge at Morfodion where David Davies started to build the first stretch of the Llanidloes & Newtown. It has survived in its original form to carry British Rail. The Llanidloes & Newtown had an easy route with only five problems in bridging; timber by canal barge to Newtown was the solution. *C. C. Green.*

Centre left: The Oswestry & Newtown was the second of the easy routes and Thomas Savin had to build only two major bridges. This one crossed the Vyrnwy. Benjamin Piercy's triple caissons, built for the second track which never materalised, and plugged with mass concrete and banded to prevent their cracking apart, carried British Rail's replacement welded girders to the end. *C. C. Green*

Below: Most of the original timber station buildings on the Oswestry & Newtown were replaced in various forms of brick and stone, but Llanymynech survived to show us both the open shelter and the timber booking office of the period. *C. C. Green*

Left: The Kerry Branch of the Oswestry & Newtown ascended the charming Mule Gorge. It was designed for single line only. The near arch crosses the river. This is a scene at Fronfaith, c 1905. *Collection C. C. Green.*

Bottom left: In a road overbridge at the East end of Newtown station, the Oswestry & Newtown gave the Cambrian its earliest example of the Brymbo Foundry's 'bulb-headed' cast iron plate girders. Others came later when the Cambrian had to replace its many unprotected road crossings with sloping ramps and bridges. *C. C. Green.*

Top right: One of the several fine bridges between Talerddig and Cemmes Road. *C. C. Green.*

Centre right: The single-line Llanfyllin Branch of the Oswestry & Newtown provided the Cambrian with one of its two 'flag' stations. Unless an intending passenger hauled up the arm showing the white disc on the red arm to the oncoming train it would not stop. The guard restored the signal. *Courtesy of M. E. M. Lloyd.*

Below: Designed by Piercy and George Owen, this splendid bridge near Cemmes Road marked the end of the difficulties of constructing the Newtown & Machynlleth and the last major use of stone taken from Talerddig cutting. The draining of the Carno bog, the crossing of the watershed and the descent of the Twymyn Gorge had been accomplished – and Davies the Contractor had arrived. *C. C. Green.*

BRYNGWYN RAILWAY STATI

" You work the Signal to stop your Tr

Top left: The Coast section's most troublesome stretch – the Friog cliffs. The ledge, it is said, was cut by sailors who could stand the heights above the rocks and surf; the men of Borth and Derwenlas, whose ships had just been laid up to rot, would have been glad to have the work. The overturned coaches were derailed in the Friog accident of 1883. *Powys Area Library Newtown.*

Centre left: For most of his railway bridges, Benjamin Piercy had evolved a standard design – 8in square baulks of timber bolt-hung from the bottom flanges of wrought iron girder sides. This bridge across A4083 outside Whitchurch was built in 1862. Daylight can be seen through the spaces between the beams. *C. C. Green.*

Bottom left: Typical of the stone station buildings of the Newtown & Machynlleth – Llanbrynmair at the turn of the century. The stationmaster's cap on the boy's head was prophetic, for Mr. W. R. Fryer was to retire as stationmaster of the station where he was born. Then nearly all young boys in rural areas wore frocks which could be handed down to the next youngest boy or girl. *Courtesy of W. R. Fryer.*

Above: The Oswestry Ellesmere & Whitchurch produced little drama in its construction. Having no stone, the idiom was brick as used in the station buildings at Bettisfield. Where its over-bridges stood on Sir John Hanmer's estates they bore his arms. *C. C. Green.*

Below: Before the Aberystwyth & Welsh Coast joined the Cambrian Thomas Savin managed to complete the isolated stretch from Aberdovey to Barmouth Junction and the Dolgelley branch as far as Penmaenpool. The road bridge was built by a private toll company which the Cambrian bought out after 1900. *G. Hayward.*

1859-1864: Early Locomotives and Rolling Stock

Below: Thomas Savin ordered six of these Sharp Stewart goods engines in his own name for the Oswestry & Newtown: *Queen* (the class name), *Prince of Wales, Hercules, Vulcan, Tubal Cain* and *Cambria.* David Davies ordered six for (to quote the makers) 'The Newton and Mackynnleth', named *Talerddig, Countess Vane, Sir Watkin, Cyfronydd, Rheiwport* and *Towyn.* Ten arrived between December 1861 and February 1863. *Rheiwport* and *Towyn* were delivered to the infant Cambrian in August 1864. All had Monsieur Giffard's new patent injector systems. *G. Grundy for Sharp Stewart.*

Bottom left: Thomas Savin's last order was for ten 2-4-0 passenger engines from Sharp Stewart. *Mazeppa* was the first to arrive at Oswestry in March 1863, followed by seven others – *Pegasus, Albion* (the class name), *Minerva, Cader Idris, Glandovey, Plynlimon* and *Rheidol.* The other two were lost to the Brecon & Merthyr. Four were delivered in March 1863 and four in March 1864. So that all the details showed up well, an engine was usually photographed for the makers in its matt grey undercoat with the maker's own lining also in matt paint, but only on the side to be photographed, as in this view of *Albion.* After this ceremony the proper colours were applied. *G. Grundy for Sharp Stewart.*

Top: Three of these fascinating little Sharp Stewart tanks were obtained by Thomas Savin, nominally for the Llanfyllin, Porthywaen and Kerry branches of the Oswestry & Newtown, in June 1863. Although depicted here around 1890, *Prometheus* has no ownership plate and apart from the trace of lining on the cabside looks very much 'as delivered'. The other two were *Plasfynnon* and *Mountaineer.* *Locomotive Publishing Co.*

Above: Six Sharp Stewart 0-4-2 engines were ordered for the Llanidloes & Newtown. Four, named *Montgomery, Llanerchydol, Leighton* and *Volunteer* (the class name), stayed in their proper area, but *Wynnstay* and *Glansevern* were lost to the Brecon & Merthyr in Savin's bankruptcy. Three were delivered in 1859, of which only *Montgomery* ever got to Llanidloes a year later when the isolated line was joined on to the Oswestry & Newtown; the other three followed at the end of 1860. Hearsay memories have it that the colour was a dark green. *Collection C. C. Green.*

Top right: This three-compartment first-class coach at Coney Crossing, Oswestry, was one of the rare contenders for the title of centenarian; it can be taken as typical of the small four-wheeled coaches of the original companies. *C. C. Green.*

Centre right: At 21 ft 6 in long, this Ashbury second-class coach did not give much in the way of legroom. Built in December 1860 for £287 it became a sleeping van in 1920 and achieved the distinction of surviving briefly in Great Western ownership. *J. P. Richards.*

Below: This 25 ft 6 in long first- and second-class was bought from Ashbury's in February 1861 for £387. Converted to a parcels van in 1915, it was condemned on sight by the Great Western as from 10 September 1922. Seen here in Herbert Jones' livery on 21 July 1904 as part of the royal train lent to Birmingham for the opening of the Elan Valley Waterworks by His Majesty King Edward VII. *L&GRP.*

Far right top: Evidence of the comfort provided for the gentry from the outset: four-wheeled first-class saloon with twin-door luggage compartment at the nearer end and a separate compartment at the further end for the servants. *G. H. W. Clifford.*

Far right bottom: The footplate crew had only wood-blocks on the tender-wheels with which to check speed and every train had to have three or more of these 'break-vans' (as they were then called). Each guard had to watch constantly from his ducket for emergency signals from in front or from behind. Note the floor-level square door leading to the dog box; dogs were not allowed in the carriages. *J. E. Cull*

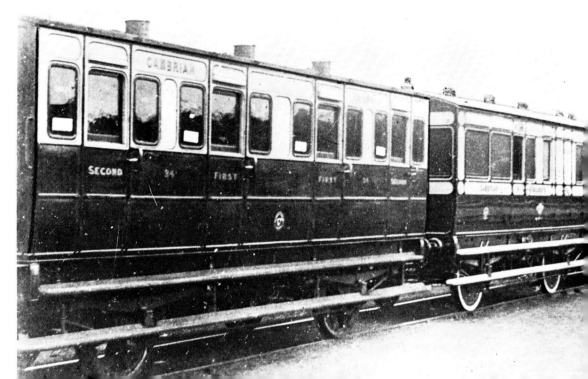

1864 – 1885:
Birth of the Cambrian Railways

The Cambrian Railways Company obtained its powers to combine and run the original four little companies on 25 July 1864. The Aberystwyth & Welsh Coast was unable to comply in time with Parliamentary Standing Orders, but it had completed its first bit of line as far as Aberystwyth five weeks before. The tenor of the first directors' report was that, whereas hitherto the aggressive policies of the great companies had always done more harm than good, from now on the new company was to be run for the benefit of its shareholders, which would also be for the benefit of the public. The principal opponent of the bill for amalgamation had been the Great Western and the new company worked in closer co-operation with the London & North Western.

After making a hefty cash contribution to aid the construction of the Aberystwyth & Welsh Coast and agreeing to operate it, the Cambrian absorbed it on 5 July 1865. By the following February Thomas Savin was bankrupt and three months after that Overend and Gurney's Bank, the greatest negotiating organisation of its time, also collapsed. The struggle to recover scattered rolling stock from the Savin empire and to complete the Coast route now began. As settlement

Below left: Mr. W. W. E. Wynn of Peniarth, Towyn is reputed to have designed the company's armorial device. By omitting the letters 'C.R. Co.' from the three dark semi-circular areas this version was evolved. It was applied to carriage sides as an ownership embellishment by William Aston some time after 1882, date of the first proven evidence of bronze-green and white, lined gold on a wider black band, as the official carriage livery. *Courtesy of George Dow*

Below: Two relics of 'The Scheme'. The initials on the ticket stand for Oswestry & Newtown and Llanidloes & Newtown Railways; the label reads Oswestry & Newtown & Llanidloes & Machynlleth Railways. Beautifully engraved copperplate letterheads of the Oswestry & Newtown and Llanidloes & Newtown Joint Railway are also known to exist. *Courtesy of W. G. Bett and Collection C. C. Green*

Right: Penhelig in 1868. The recently-built embankment and road bridges, both of the underhung timber deck type, and No.4 Tunnel indicate the completion of the link with the rest of the Cambrian from Dovey Junction to Aberdovey Station on 14 August 1867, and the end of the *Elizabeth's* ferry service. *Courtesy of Mrs. C. F. Ellis.*

Bottom right: The men who managed the Cambrian at first.
Standing centre: Mr George Owen the Engineer, formerly assistant to Benjamin Piercy during the construction, 1864-98.
Standing right: Mr. Henry Cattle, Traffic Manager, 1870-1878.
Seated left: Mr. Alexander Walker, Locomotive Superintendant – formerly superintendant to Thomas Savin's varied locomotive stud, 1866-1879.
Seated centre: Mr George Lewis, Secretary & General Manager, 1864-1882.
Seated right: Mr H. C. Corfield, Solicitor. *The Story of the Cambrian.*

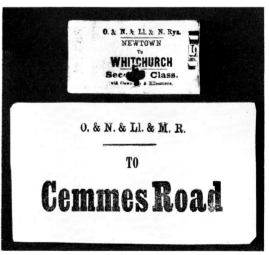

proceeded and engines were conceded beyond dispute to the Cambrian, one can imagine the satisfaction with which the little brass plates with blue infilled grounds reading 'CAMBRIAN RAILWAY No. etc.' were affixed.

The odds were too great and the new company went bankrupt on 15 February 1868, with the deputy-chairman Captain Robert D. Pryce as receiver. What was known as 'The Scheme' kept things going uneasily until the 'old constitution' was restored on 1 January 1879; then matters finally collapsed and the Cambrian was bankrupt again on 12 July 1884. This time an able and ruthless professional, John Conacher, who had been secretary since 1882, took over as receiver. He reduced no less than seventy different forms of stock to ten and re-organised the capital liabilities down to under £6 million. The main trouble was on paper, for as a working railway the Cambrian was not doing too badly, so he was able to satisfy the creditors and get the company discharged from bankruptcy by 18 February 1885.

Above: The stations of the Coast route were mainly of wood and several were replaced by brick. Dyffryn Ardudwy is typical of the latter. Note the water-proofed roughcast and tile-hung gable – attempts to make the house more habitable in westerly gales. *C. C. Green*

Below: The principal feature of the coast route, the original 'cock-and-draw' or 'overdraw' bridge across the Mawddach channel close to Barmouth. The gentleman who knew the bridge could not be built, and swore to eat the first engine to cross it, was dumped down at a table in Barmouth and asked if he wanted it roast or boiled – possibly some time in October, 1867, when a proper train service replaced a leisurely horse-drawn carriage that had worked since 3 June that year. *Collection C. C. Green.*

Top right: No. 45 *Rhiewport* came in for an odd treatment of the ownership marking – 'CAMBRIAN RAIL CY' on the centre splasher and No. 45 on the leading splasher. With No. 46 *Towyn* she was delivered to the Cambrian direct only a month after the company had been formed – perhaps this

was the reason. Like the six Newtown & Machynlleth engines, she has a six-wheeled tender. Later these were swapped about with the four-wheeled tenders according to working needs. Two more, Nos. 51 *Snowdon* and 52 *Harlech*, arrived in 1865. A further four Nos. 1 *Victoria*, 2 (soon renumbered 4) *Alexandra*, 6 *Marquis* and 10 *Marchioness* were added in 1872/73. *Locomotive Publishing Co.*

Right: Sharp Stewart goods No. 27 *Cambria* at Machynlleth c 1870, now painted in unlined black; only the brass plate above the centre axle proclaims that it belongs to the new Cambrian. The other eleven had become Nos. 11 *Queen*, 12 *Prince of Wales*, 19 *Hercules*, Brecon & Merthyr 3 *Vulcan*, 26 *Tubal Cain*, 34 *Talerddig*, 35 *Countess Vane*, 39 *Sir Watkin*, 40 *Cyfronydd*, 45 *Rhiewport* and 46 *Towyn*. *Locomotive Publishing Co.*

Bottom right: No 30 *Albion* with her plate of Cambrian ownership. The other seven had become Nos 28 *Mazeppa*, 29 *Pegasus*, 31 *Minerva*, 41 *Cader Idris*, 42 *Glandovey*, 43 *Plynlimon* and 44 *Rheidol*. *Courtesy of Ifor Higgon.*

Above: An inaugural present for the infant Cambrian – eight of these London & North Western style first/second composites already on order were delivered in July and August 1864. No. 76 was to run until the Great Western detected her in September 1923; at least they photographed her before she was scrapped. She is seen here at Blodwell Junction in post-1899 livery. *L&GRP*.

Left: Built by the Midland Wagon Company around 1864 for £62.50, this dumb-buffered wagon survived until 1900. A new wagon took its number in 1904. *Cambrian Official*.

Bottom left: The brigantine *Charlotte* of Aberdovey (Thomas Daniel, Master) painted entering Leghorn in 1864. The directors feared that red and green railway signal lamps could be mistaken by the navigators of these beautiful little ships for the port and starboard lights of other vessels, so causing them to be wrecked through standing too close inshore. Cambrian railway signal lights were therefore violet for danger and white for all clear. *Courtesy of Mrs C. F. Ellis.*

Right: Guard Cudworth. Right through to the 1890s the servants who directly attended the public bore collar patches of identification – 'PORTER' or 'GUARD' and senior staff wore the silver feathers emblem. *The Story of the Cambrian.*

Below: The Cambrian took four more Sharp Stewart passenger engines at the end of 1865. Nos. 53 *Gladstone*, 54 *Palmerston*, 55 *Treflach*, and 56 *Whittington* were a new departure in naming, two being national politicians instead of directors or their homes. See how carefully the jet pilots of their day have groomed their machine for its photograph with symmetrical rag-dabbing on the tender and side-sheet. Oswestry, c 1870. *Courtesy of Ifor Higgon.*

Top right: Oswestry, 1870. This photograph merits close study. The six wagons in the background rake are: (from left to right): an outside-framed sprung buffered wagon, with traces of small lettering; a dumb-buffered drop-door wagon with no trace of lettering; a similar, slightly higher wagon with traces of small lettering; a short box wagon with three words along the second plank down; a vehicle similar to the second wagon, but definitely lettered with three words, centrally; and a sprung low-sided wagon loaded with rough stone. On the extreme left is a dumb-buffered Cambrian two-plank, fixed-side wagon, which was shunted into place during the lengthy time exposure (about two minutes) that was needed to create the image on the slow wet plate. The first of the nearer pair of wagons carries a tarpaulin lettered 'CAMBRIAN RAILWAY 507'. The wagon on the extreme right is a Cambrian drop-side with raised ends. The four-wheeled box-van is one of the 'break-vans' delivered in 1864 by the Metropolitan Railway Carriage & Wagon Co. The five compartment outside-framed Parliamentary (the term was just about still in use, as evidenced by a timetable of the time) third is another acquisition of 1864 from the Metropolitan Carriage & Wagon Co. 'Compartment' is a nominal term only, for the divisions ceased at seat level. Here the number looks like 86 in a plain garland. The colour is probably brown. Under the end of the timber a short dumb-buffered fixed-side wagon is serving as a match-truck. *Courtesy of Ifor Higgon.*

Below: 2-4-0 No. 43 *Plynlimon* poses with an outside-framed five-compartment Parliamentary third, an open interior four-compartment third, a first/second composite, an outside-framed three-compartment Parliamentary brake third and a sliding-door roader parcels brake-van. The other engine is 0-6-0 No 6 *Marquis.* Aberystwyth, c 1875. *Courtesy of Ifor Higgon.*

Above: No 42 *Glandovey* with the crude tongued and grooved-board front and sides fitted to the spectacle plates in the 1870's to give a little protection to the crews. There were still no roofs to form even elementary cabs. Seen at Barmouth, c 1888. *Collection C. C. Green.*

Above: In May 1866 three of a new sort were received from Sharp Stewart & Co, Nos. 57 *Maglona*, 58 *Gladys* and 59 *Seaham*. Note the dumb-buffered wagon and the intriguing fragment of an outside-framed open but roofed cattle truck. Llanfyllin, c 1890. *L&GRP.*

Below: Sharp Stewart 0-6-0 tank No 13, bought in February 1875 for banking duties between Machynlleth and Talerddig. It was decided that she should henceforth bear the name of her place of work and 0-6-0 No 34 *Talerddig* gave up her nameplates and received a grander pair , *Cader Idris*, which were lying spare in Oswestry works. This had been brought about by the realisation that the name and title of the chairman's wife was borne by – *a goods engine!*

Accordingly, 0-6-0 No 35 *Countess Vane* was downgraded to *Castell Deudraeth* and the 2-4-0 passenger engine No 41 *Cader Idris* took the title, the company thereby purging itself of *lése majesté*. No 13 ended her days as the Workshop Engine at Oswestry until 1920, after 45 years of service, with little alteration besides the new chimney and steel brake-blocks. Even then her service was not finished, for her boiler went to raise steam for the Aberystwyth pumping station and her frames and motion were bolted down inside Oswestry Works to drive additional machinery. To the last, Oswestry wasted nothing. *Locomotive Publishing Co.*

Above: No. 59 *Seaham* halted at Vrondirion near Dolgelley, c 1882. The leading van is Oswestry & Newtown brake No. 101 lettered 'PASSENGERS LUGGAGE'. The second coach is an Ashbury-built 1st/2nd composite No 47 and is still carrying an earlier device on a shield-shaped mounting. The remaining coaches are Cambrian outside-framed Parliamentary stock of 1864. Colours are probably cream and brown *John Thomas; Courtesy of The National Library of Wales.*

Top right: In August 1878 two of a new class to become known as the 'Small Sharp Stewarts' were delivered. They were virtually extended and improved 2-4-0s, and the rebuilds of the latter were strongly reminiscent of their new cousins in outline. These were the first engines to carry the company's device and the last to be given valence-mounted ownership plates and names, which were those of great statesmen – Nos 16 *Beaconsfield*, seen here at Oswestry in 1891, and 17 *Hartington*. Eight years elapsed before the Cambrian could afford two more, Nos. 20 and 21 (the Cambrian's first vacuum-braked engines), and Nos. 50 and 60 followed thirteen years later in 1891. *Locomotive Publishing Co.*

Centre right: William Aston reported in 1882 that cabs similar to those fitted to 'the new engines' could be made in the works for £13 and these were added as engines came into Oswestry for other work. This haphazard method of selection caused the job to spread into the 1890s. *The National Library of Wales.*

Right: The new livery, probably introduced by William Aston as his first change around 1882, was black with a light blue-grey lining flanked both sides with equally wide signal red – a rather flamboyant style. It is seen on Sharp Stewart goods 0-6-0 No. 12 *Prince of Wales*. Within the previous three years the company had taken on three more of this type, all bargains. Sharps had built them in 1875 for the Furness, which could not afford them, so in 1878 Sharps offered two as unused for £1,765 each, barely half what they would have cost if ordered new. These became Nos. 14 *Broneirion* and 15 *Glansevern*, and at last Mrs. Ann Warburton Owen had her long-promised named engine. The third Furness 'reject' went to the Denbigh Ruthin & Corwen Railway, which soon became London and North Western property. She was later offered to the Cambrian, who bought this, their final example of the design, for £1,125 in 1879 and made her No. 18 *Orleton*. In 1879, too, Alexander Walker retired and William Aston became Locomotive Superintendent. *Cambrian Official.*

Above: In 1882 the first two six-wheelers were built in Oswestry Works. They were 28ft 6in long five-compartment thirds, costing £300 each. More followed next year, built by the Metropolitan Railway, Carriage, and Wagon Co. for a lower price of £260 each. One of the first pair, No. 116, was made into a parcels van in 1918 and appeared in the Great Western's 'rolling museum' series of photographs taken in 1923. *GWR Official.*

Below: No. 37 *Mountaineer*, with the new lining and Cambrian Railway ownership plate. The other two of this type became Nos. 36 *Plasfynnon* and 38 *Prometheus*. *Locomotive Publishing Co.*

Above: Dolgelley train at Barmouth Junction in the early 1880s. The locomotive is a Sharp Stewart 0-4-2 of the 'Volunteer' class running tender-first. The first coach is an outside-framed parliamentary brake-third with plain instead of birdcage roof; the second is a first/second composite of 1864; and the third is a four-compartment third. The last is a very intriguing specimen indeed. It has the oval-panelled doors of the three-compartment first at Coney Crossing pictured earlier and was possibly first-luggage – first-first; it is still in one of the early overall brown liveries. *Collection G. Dow.*

Below: The first of the Cambrian's three 'classic' accidents – the Friog of 1 January 1883. About 30 tons of stones and soil from the toll road above fell on to the track and overturned No. 29 *Pegasus* onto the beach. The driver and fireman were killed, but the leading coach – the outside-framed coach on its side above – was empty and most of the passengers in the four-vehicle train were in the third coach, which never left the rails. *Collection C. C. Green.*

1885 – 1899: The Cambrian grows up

The build-up to a high standard of smartness and service now began. First, the carriage stock had to be upgraded to attract passengers to make holiday journeys to the coast. That meant more of the new six-wheel thirds for a start, and some new luggage locker composites for through running. More goods stock was acquired too. Now the years of attrition were over. The locomotives and carriages were greatly increased in number and much improved in standard and appearance.

Above: Alfred Aslett, General Manager from 1891-1899 – a conscientious autocrat who carried on the process of improvement started by Connacher. *The Story of the Cambrian.*

Left: One of the two men who set the Cambrian to rights – John Connacher, the ruthless professional who was Secretary from 1882 and General Manager from 1890. He went to the North British Railway as General Manager in 1891, but came back to the Cambrian as Chairman, 1909-1911. *The Story of the Cambrian.*

Above: No. 1 *Victoria* before 22 April 1886, resplendent in a trial lining of red edged blue-grey. *Courtesy of Ifor Higgon.*

Below: Mid-Wales Kitson 0-6-0 No. 12 at Newbridge-on-Wye. The lame duck that the Mid-Wales had become was taken over in 1888. The Cambrian acquired ten of these worn-out lightweights and managed to concoct four runners, which were numbered 25, 32, 33 and 47. Only No. 33, combining Mid-Wales No. 7's frame and No. 8's boiler, lasted past 1895 to be scrapped in 1904. The livery at first was dark green and the lining, which curves in at the corners, was said to have been broad black edged gold: with the beautiful lake-terra cotta hue of the carriages, the Mid Wales when new must have looked magnificent. *Courtesy of Ifor Higgon.*

Top: Mid-Wales Kitson 0-4-2 No. 2 of 1864 outside Builth Wells Stores with her new oval cast brass number plate, slightly smaller than the old one, now reading Cambrian Railways No. 2. Originally there were six of this type, of which four came to the Cambrian as Nos 2, 22, 23 and 24. All were scrapped by 1905. The single curved lining, probably gold, was the Mid-Wales' last livery. Old Cambrian memories recalled that she was painted black, but one instance of an 0-4-2 in brick-red was recorded by H. Holcroft. *Cambrian Official.*

Above: Mid-Wales Sharp Stewart 0-6-0 No. 9 at Llanidloes about 1885. She and her sister No. 10, built in 1873, became Cambrian Nos 48 and 49 as additions to the 'Queen' class – the best engines the Cambrian gained out of the takeovers. The livery shown here may have been dark green or even plain black. *Courtesy of Ifor Higgon.*

Right: The Mid-Wales bridges were devised so that all could be assembled from only eleven basic components. The spidery multi-span ones, fine for the light Kitson engines and short trains, gave much trouble later on; all had bracings added and many had to be encased in solid concrete piers to arrest their downstream 'creep'. The middle of 'Q' bridge across the Ithon was noticeably further to the west than its ends before it was dismantled. This is 'A' Bridge over the River Dulas. *C. C. Green.*

Above: The route to Brecon was scenically one of the loveliest runs any railway had to offer the traveller, winding as it did along the steep-sided valleys of the Dulas, the Marteg and the Wye. This is 'N' Bridge over the River Wye, south of Rhayader. *C. C. Green.*

Below: By 1888 the old quay at Aberdovey had been much improved and it is interesting to see the outer rail running within a foot or two from the edge. The brig *Excelsior* is unloading timber into Cambrian wagons about 1898. *Courtesy of J. Parry.*

Top: This fanciful print of two steam brigantines, one flying the Dragon of Wales at the jackstaff, some old advertising notices, and a book of cabin tickets have survived to mark the Cambrian's short-lived venture into shipping with the *Liverpool* and the *Cambria* in 1889. By getting the afterguard of the *Liverpool* drunk, so that they mistook Cardigan Bay outer buoy for the inner and lost a tide, thereby necessitating the slaughter of an entire boatload of thirst-crazed cattle on Towyn beach, the London & North Western agent at Waterford put paid to the Aberdovey and Waterford Steamship Company within a few months of its first sailings. A second attempt with a better ship, the *Magnetic,* which was succeeded by the *Electric,* also failed. *Collection C. C. Green.*

Above: The second pair of Small Sharp Stewart 4-4-0s, Nos 20 and 21 (seen here at Oswestry in March 1889), were delivered in July 1886. The lighter colour of the tender sheeting is an illusion caused by rag-dabbing. The device on the leading splasher was to become a constant feature on the passenger engines from now on. *Collection C. C. Green.*

Below: No 53, ex-*Gladstone,* at Oswestry in March 1889. Mr Aston had set about improving both the appearance and performance of the little 2-4-0 passenger engines. The Sharp Stewart choker chimneys were scrapped and his new chimneys improved the blast and steaming. Brakes on the engine as well as on the tender were worked by vacuum and required an injector pipe along the boiler into the smokebox,

so the nameplates had to go. To compensate, the leading splasher has been sheeted over to carry the device. *Locomotive Publishing Co.*

Top: No. 54 ex-*Palmerston* also in renovated condition at Oswestry in March 1889. With the blue-grey lining edged signal red and all brasswork polished the 'Albion' class now cut quite a dash. E. L. Ahrons wrote in his series on 19th century railway working that he had difficulty in understanding how the Cambrian maintained its services. The returns for 1888 showed an *average* working day, locomotive and crew, of 13 hours, with only two engines at a time in works for lengthy repairs. *Locomotive Publishing Co.*

Above: No 9 ex-*Volunteer* at Oswestry in March 1889 with a proper cab and an Aston chimney, vacuum and steam brakes

working on the driving wheels, and steam sanding – the only one of her class to attain all four refinements. With No 8 (ex-*Leighton*) she was scrapped in 1899. The other two of the class No 5 (ex-*Montgomery*) and No 7 (ex-*Llanerchydol*) went four years earlier. *Locomotive Publishing Co.*

Below: In December 1888 No 15 ex-*Glansevern* emerged from the works with a new boiler on a higher centre-line and working at a higher pressure. In this form 16 of the old 'Queen' class became invaluable little machines of considerable versatility. As yet she still has brakes on the tender only and gravity sanding, but she bears the first cast-brass number plate to replace her valence-mounted ownership plate. Seen here at Oswestry in March 1889. *Locomotive Publishing Co.*

Top: No. 48, one of the Mid-Wales Sharp Stewarts, was the second to be 'done up' in March 1889. However, the goods engines must have been kept strictly to such duties as they still had no engine brakes. The Ramsbottom safety valves which were to become standard on the Cambrian show more clearly here. *Locomotive Publishing Co.*

Above: No. 6 *Marquis* at Oswestry in March 1889, still with only her matchboard weather protection. Some of the class had these fitments added between 1885 and 1888, but others received proper cabs as their first improvement. Note the elaborately panelled lining on the tender. *Locomotive Publishing Co.*

Top right: No. 51 *Snowdon* at Oswestry in March 1889. Her nameplates were removed before the month was out following a general policy decision to abandon names on locomotives. *Locomotive Publishing Co.*

Centre right: 'Queen' class No 52 *Harlech*, at Oswestry around 1889, shows an unusual arrangement of nameplate and makers plate. *Courtesy of Ifor Higgon.*

Right: Montgomery Station c 1890, with an 'Albion' class 2-4-0 on a London & North Western train. Also seen is original wagon No. 1067 with dumb-buffers, in light grey with black iron-work and solebars. *John Thomas, Courtesy The National Library of Wales.*

Top to bottom: Llanfihangel geneu'r Glyn, later Llandre, c 1890, with a 'Queen' class 0-6-0 on the right. Already an early four-wheeled coach has been 'grounded' by the station as a store of some sort. The private owner wagons are: Lewis Edwards No.2; dumb-buffered Rd. Williamson & Sons No.134; and William Morgan No.3 *John Thomas Courtesy The National Library of Wales.*

A posed scene of the period, taken at Towyn in 1891. The train is even placed on the wrong line so that the glare from the sea on the right is assisting and not hindering the cameraman. Note the covered-in state of the rails – as yet there is no foot-bridge. The end window reads 'SECOND CLASS WAITING ROOM' *Courtesy of Mrs. C. F. Ellis.*

In 1890 Nos 56 ex-*Whittington* (seen here at Oswestry in 1891) and 31 ex-*Minerva* were the first of the 'Albions' to receive the new higher-pressure boilers similar to those fitted to the 'Queen' class; the 'Albions' got steam sanding as well. Despite shorter chimneys, they still retained their dashing look. *Locomotive Publishing Co.*

No 1, formerly *Victoria*, at Oswestery in 1891. She did not lose her archaic look until rebuilt in 1893. Nobody seems to have raised any objection to the name of the reigning monarch gracing a goods engine. *Locomotive Publishing Co.*

Above: Ellesmere Station provided offices for the Oswestry, Ellesmere & Whitchurch and later for the Wrexham & Ellesmere Railways. Here, in 1892, the Cambrian made its mark in the annals of trade union history. John Hood, the stationmaster, had given evidence before a Parliamentary Committee enquiring into over-long hours worked by railwaymen (a 60 hour working week was nothing unusual and only the Welsh regard for Sunday observance kept the hours worked from being even more). He was sacked and for this breach of privilege the Chairman, General Manager, and Board were publicly admonished by the Speaker at the Bar of the House of Commons. The Secretary of the Amalgamated Society of Railway Servants of the United Kingdom denounced the Cambrian, saying that 'little railways were a gigantic mistake', and the Labour press thundered 'Cambrian Tyranny'. But such was the power of management in those days that Mr Hood stayed sacked. Later he achieved a long career of honourable public service in local administration at Ellesmere. *C. C. Green.*

Below: No 4, formerly *Alexandra*, after 5 May 1891. She was the fourth of the Sharp Stewart 0-6-0s to be modernised with a new boiler – and then they became really up-to-date. Exhaust ejector pipes and six-wheel brakes have also been added. *Locomotive Publishing Co.*

Below: Any one of these engines would have worked Noyadd Sidings from Railway No.1 of the Birmingham Corporation Waterworks. In order they are *Elan, Coel, Calettwr, Rhiwnant, Nant Gwyllt* and *Claerwen*. All were built by Manning Wardle & Co., except for *Nant Gwyllt*, which was a Hunslet. Two more Hunslets, *Methan and Marchnant*, were mostly working away at the top end of the valley – sometimes even cut off when tracks were severed and re-aligned. All took their names from streams which flow into the reservoirs. Noyadd Sidings, just south of Rhayader Tunnel, were worked by Cambrian engines which delivered construction materials for the reservoirs and took away empty wagons; the Birmingham engines returned the empties and took away the full on the last stages of their tortuous journeys. The engines were kept from meeting by an agreed time embargo. *Courtesy of J. Hamer.*

Bottom right: A close-up of *Coel*, which according to Manning Wardle was assembled from standard parts off a written specification without a drawing. The gentleman on the right is G. N Yourdi, the Graeco-Irish Resident Engineer. His 'saloon' is an ex-Mid-Wales brake-van. *Courtesy of Birmingham Water Dept.*

Top left: A pause from shunting duties at Minfford about 1891. *Queen* has lost her nameplate and, unlike the rebuilt engines, probably had not changed in appearance any more when she was scrapped in 1899. The embankment behind carried the narrow-gauge Festiniog Railway and the track against the bank on the right served the Maenofferen Slate Quarry exchange sidings on top of the bank. The diminutive trucks were worked into position for unloading via a grid of tiny turntables. Behind the camera the track curved down to form three parallel sidings leading to the goods shed. The line coming away to the left past the signal served first the coal-drops, whence the Festiniog received its supply of prime-mover fuel, and then descended in a long curve to get alongside more narrow-gauge exchange sidings. The main line is down out of sight behind the signal. Altogether Minfford was a difficult station, both for halting a train and for shunting. *Courtesy of Ifor Higgon.*

Centre left: An Aberystwyth-bound local train at Machynlleth in the early 1890s with an 'austerity' Oswestry-built third class coach leading, then a diminutive saloon composite with an end-luggage compartment, another third and a six-wheeled brake third. The 'Albion' class 2-4-0 is still unrebuilt except for a cab, covered-in wheel splasher and a new chimney. One envies the photographer the full-hearted co-operation of the assembled station staff and passengers. *J. Thomas, Courtesy of The National Library of Wales.*

Top right: In 1893, with only six reasonably new engines out of a total stock of 59 – and of these a further 17 badly needed rebuilding and nine were past it – Mr. Aston brought out his 61 class, later known as the 'Large Sharp Stewarts'; 20 were delivered in the six years to 1898. Nos 61-68 were delivered in 1893 in various experimental liveries, which were soon discarded, but the 1894 batch, Nos 69-72, showed a fresh

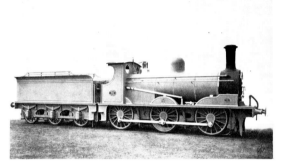

arrangement; there was a device only on the splasher and a cast brass numberplate, both items which were thereafter standard. The pronounced lead of the bogie, well in advance of the main weight of the cylinders and boiler, made the 61 class very steady runners and they were esteemed very highly by their crews. *L & GRP.*

Above: In 1894 Nos 73-77, the first five of these handsome little engines, were delivered by Neilson Reid & Co. who delivered two more, Nos 87 and 88, in 1899. They took their designer's name and became the 'Aston Goods'. Unlike those of any other Cambrian engines, their sand-boxes were faired into the leading splashers; Nos 78-80, built by the Vulcan Foundry in 1895, had much larger ones. *Neilson Reid & Co.*

BIRMINGHAM ONION FAIR, SEPTEMBER 28th, 29th, and

On Thursday, September 28th, 1893,
CHEAP 1 DAY AND 3 DAYS TICKETS
WILL BE ISSUED TO

BIRMINGHAM

AS UNDER :—

From	Times of Starting	Third Class Fares there and back.	
	a.m.	DAY TRIP	THREE DAYS
Pwllheli	dep. 6 0		
Afon Wen	,, 6 15		
Criccieth	,, 6 21		
Portmadoc	,, 6 30		
Minffordd	,, 6 34	6s.	10s. 6d.
Penrhyndeudraeth	,, 6 38		
Talsarnau	,, 6 42		
Harlech	,, 6 50		
Llanbedr and Pensarn	,, 6 58		
Dyffryn	,, 7 8		
Barmouth	,, 7 20		
Town	,, 7 50	5s.	9s. 6d.
Aberdovey	,, 8 0		
Aberystwyth	,, 9 0		
Bow Street	,, 7 50		
Llanfihangel	,, 54		10s. 6d.
Borth	,, 7 49		
Ynyslas	,, 8 4		
Glandovey	,, 8 14		
Machynlleth	,, 9 50	5s.	9s. 6d.
Cemmes Road	,, 8 43		
Llanbrynmair	,, 8 53		
Carno	,, 9 10		
Pontdolgoch	,, 9 20	5s.	9s.
Caersws	,, 9 26		

A Through Coach will be run from Aberystwyth, Forden, and intermediate Stations to Birmingham.

Children under 3 years of age, Free : above 3 and under 12 years of age, Half-price.

Day Trip Passengers return from Birmingham (New Street) at 11-15 p.m. on date of issue of the Ticket.

Passengers holding Three Days' Tickets return from Birmingham at 11-30 a.m. on September 29th or 30th.

The Cambrian Railways Company have 26 Rail and Coach Excursions DAILY, through unsurpassed Mountain, Coast, River, and Lake Scenery.

Excursionists are recommended to see the Cambrian Railways Programme of Rail and Coach Tours, which may be had on application at any of their Stations, or from the undersigned.

"Picturesque Wales" (Illustrated), the Official Guide Book to the Cambrian Railways, edited by Mr Godfrey Turner, price 6d., and new Pamplet "Where to Stay and What to See"? (Illustrated), price 2d., containing information respecting Hotels, Inns, Farm Houses, and Country Lodgings in Wild and Picturesque Wales, can be obtained at the Bookstalls, or on application at the Company's Offices or Stations.

The Tickets are not transferable, and will only be available to and from the stations named upon them, and by the Trains specified on the bills.

The issuing of Through Tickets is subject to the conditions and regulations referred to in the Time Tables, Bills, and Notices of the respective Companies, on whose Railway they are available, and the holder by accepting a Through Ticket agrees that the respective Companies are not to be liable for any loss or damage, injury, delay, or detention caused or arising off their respective Railways. The contract and liability of each Company are limited to its own Railway.

Tickets, bills, and every information to be had at the above-named stations.

Company's Offices,
Oswestry, September, 1893.

ALFRED ASLETT,
Secretary and General Manager.

No. 364—D.   Edwin Poole, "Express" Office, Caxton Buildings, Brecon.

Left: A faded and stained excursion bill of this period found in the roof of Barmouth Junction. *Collection C. C. Green*

Below: The old smithy at Oswestry works. The two steam hammers at the back were supplied to the Oswestry & Newtown Railway and as late as 1964 it was still possible to lay hands on a huge spanner marked O & N. Although relatively small, these works had rebuilt all 12 'Albions', 16 of the 'Queens' and the three Seaham tanks between 1890 and 1897. *E. Colclough.*

Top right: This early Kodak snapshot taken about 1895 of No 37 *Mountaineer* at Abermule, shows hazily the author's uncle enjoying a brief moment of a small boy's dream. More important, it shows the round-topped opening, closed by two half-flap doors, in the cab rear through which coal was handed down from the Kerry branch coal-store – a wagon parked against a buffer-stop in Abermule. *Courtesy of S. D. Moore.*

Centre right: William Aston's 0-4-4 tanks, built by Nasmyth Wilson & Co, were neat effective units which served well both on the Wrexham and Ellesmere and on the Dollgelley branches, often moving quite heavy trains on these short hauls. Nos 3, 5 and 7 were delivered in 1895 and 8, 9 and 23 in 1899. No 5 is seen as new, running in 'broad Aston' livery. Note the 'ISCA FOUNDRY, ENGINEERS, NEWPORT MON' plate on the turntable undertruss, and the oil lamp on the right and the addition of the neat little tool box. *Courtesy of R. E. Thomas.*

Bottom right: The second of the Sharp Stewart 2-4-0 tanks to be handsomely rebuilt, No. 59 *Seaham* (named for the chairman's son, Viscount Seaham) figured in this official photograph of 1894. It has new boiler, Aston chimney, Ramsbottom safety valves, steam sanding and a full lining-out. *Cambrian Official.*

Above: On 11 June 1897 the Cambrian had the second of its 'classic' accidents, when a Sunday School excursion returning to Royton after a happy day at the seaside left the rails at Welshhampton. The company maintained that the leading van, a Lancashire & Yorkshire four-wheeler, was running rough. The van's owners declared indignantly that anything would run rough on Cambrian track. Colonel Yorke, the Board of Trade inspector, found the track to be in an inadequate condition for fast running and that 11 children had been killed in a tumbling, sliding disorder which should never have happened. More young lives could have been saved if some of the wreckage could have been raised only a little, and as part of its expiatory actions the Board of Directors ordered that henceforth all engines should carry heavy lifting jacks. *Courtesy of Paul Tims.*

Right: In August 1896 the company started working the Van Railway (opened in 1871) and so once again had Manning Wardle saddle tanks on the strength. Van Railway No 2 of 1877, became Cambrian No 25 and the older No 1 of 1871 Cambrian No 22, but being in poor condition the latter was scrapped only three years later – and to confuse the record No 22's ornate Doric safety valve column was put on to No 25. Ex-Van Railway No 2, now Cambrian No 25, is seen in the broad Aston livery at the Van Mine about 1898. The collection of free ballast from the old mine spoil-heaps proved a disaster; the metallic ore dusted badly and before it had finally settled it would badly grind away a low-slung valve-gear's brass bearing metal. After that the engineer's department had to be more careful about selection and use. *Courtesy of W. R. Bradley.*

Centre right: The Van carriages were no assets – of the two this was the better one. It is unlikely that either ran much after 1893 when the line became derelict. Pwll-glas had the typical station-cum-crossing keeper's house and signals, seen here in 1908. In its prime the Van lead mine was rich and profitable, but the Cambrian did not take over the railway until all this was in the past. *G. M. Perkins.*

54

Top: Welshpool on 25 June 1896 as No 68 takes over the Great Western Royal Train, standing at the London & North Western platform to take Edward, Prince of Wales, to Aberystwyth for installation as Chancellor of the University. *Courtesy of Ifor Higgon.*

Bottom left: Four more Class 61 came from Sharp Stewart in May 1895 as Nos 81-84, but the last four of the class, Nos 32, 47, 85 and 86, were built by Robert Stephenson & Co. and were delivered during 1897 and 1898. Note the larger Stephenson plate now on the leading splasher. *Real Photographs.*

Above: An Aston bogie tricomposite carriage at Barmouth in 1898 in Aston's dignified bronze-green and white livery with black banding and central gold stripe round all the panel mouldings. The two devices proclaim that it belongs to the Cambrian Railways. Detailed examination of the over-exposed negative reveals that the compartment wording on the doors is three thirds, two seconds, and one first and that the coach is No 274. As yet 'CAMBRIAN RAILWAYS' does not appear on the panels above the windows. The route board reads 'CAMBRIAN RAILWAYS MANCHESTER BARMOUTH' in red, with some unreadable gold lettering in the middle – probably 'THROUGH CARRIAGE'. *L&GRP.*

Far left: Signals controlling main-line movements had Chance Bros. 'ruby-gold' glasses for danger. Fine gold-dust in the glass gave a ruby violet effect as in Victorian wine-glasses, classed in the rule-books as violet. The all-clear aspect was plain white glass. Shunt arms had pale magenta glass which photographed white. All-clear for shunt movements was pale green. These signals are at Llynclys Junction. *L&GRP.*

Left: A typical Cambrian gantry construction at Barmouth Junction North Box, surviving in 1918 as built except for the 1914-18 wartime replacement of pale green for all-clear on the main-line arm. *H. W. Burman.*

Far bottom left' A typical Cambrian point indicator lamp at Llanbrynmair. The aspects were pale green for set straight and 'ruby-gold' or magenta for set to turn. *C. C. Green.*

Bottom left: Signals with arms slotted into the post were being replaced by the orthodox externally-pivotted arm type. Tall signals in exposed sites had wound-up lamps to save climbing. The Cambrian never departed from the painted disc on signal arms, except on distants, which bore an acute fish-tail stripe. *H. W. Burman.*

Above: Aston's last six-wheeled carriages, brought into service in 1899, appeared from the works in C. S. Denniss's new brighter livery. This is brake 3rd No 78. *Cambrian Official.*

Below: A typical warehouse crane at Llanbrynmair. Note triangulation of support up in the roof beams. *C. C. Green.*

1899 – 1914:
The Best Years

The Best Years had come. 1899 was the end of an era; the old Cambrian men had all retired and William Aston left in that year, tired and ill from frequent brushes with the old General Manager, Alfred Aslett. C. S. Denniss, the new General Manager, brought in as Locomotive Superintendent Herbert Jones, who would support him in his drive to publicise the Cambrian and the seaside resorts it served.

CAMBRIAN RAILWAYS.

THROUGH LAVATORY CARRIAGES

BY

Special Service of Express Trains,

RUN AS UNDER:

LONDON (Euston)
To Aberystwyth via Welshpool 9 §30, 11 0 a.m.
and 2 35 p.m.
To Barmouth via Welshpool, 9 30 and 11 0 a.m.
To Criccieth via Welshpool. 9 30 and 11 0 a.m.

LIVERPOOL (Lime Street)
To Aberystwyth via Whitchurch, 8 15, 10 30,
a.m., 12 10 and 3 25 p.m.
From Aberystwyth via Whitchurch, 8 45 a.m.,
12 5 noon, and 2 15 p.m.

☞ GREAT ACCELERATION
Between **Leeds, Sheffield,**
LIVERPOOL, MANCHESTER,
and other LARGE TOWNS in
LANCASHIRE AND & YORKSHIRE
ABERYSTWYTH, BARMOUTH,
AND THE
Cambrian Coast,

Top left: Charles Sherwood Denniss, the forceful and publicity-conscious General Manager who made every effort to make the Cambrian a popular and paying railway. *The Story of the Cambrian*

Far left: Herbert Edward Jones, the locomotive superintendant who helped Denniss to cut costs; the old perfectionist ways of William Aston had to go. Occasionally Herbert Jones' enthusiasm for his craft ran away with him, as one delightful story testifies. Going to a conference of the Institute of Mechanical Engineers he entertained two fellow-travellers who joined him at Reading with a dissertation on railway matters in general and on the art of designing locomotives in particular. It was only on arrival at the meeting place that it became apparent to him that his

courteous listeners were the famous Great Western designers William Dean and George Jackson Churchward. *The Railway Magazine.*

Left: A. J. Collin, MICE, a competent and qualified civil engineer who only stayed three years, His successor, G. C. MacDonald, stayed with the company until 1922. *Commerce.*

Above and top: Today some of Denniss's publicity would be open to mischievous *double entendre*. The Victorians were much too dignified and satisfied with their efforts to detect such possibilities. *Collection C. C. Green*

Above: Literally 'mouthwatering prices' – until one remembers the going rate of pay of 7 old pence (a little under 3p) per hour for an unskilled labourer and 1s 3d (just over 6p) for an artificer. The price for a lunch basket went down to 2s 6d (12½p) by 1915. *Collection C.C. Green.*

Right: The wide range of pre-printed tickets held at Cambrian stations makes an interesting study. *Courtesy of W. G. Bett.*

Bottom right: Besides its own internal luggage labels, the Cambrian printed very many exotic outsiders and its label-racks must have been enormous. *Collection C. C. Green.*

Below: Denniss and Jones' first innovation was a new livery. For the engines it meant a lining of middle chrome yellow edged fine signal-red. The device remained on the splasher as before, but a magnificent crest, the Prince of Wales feathers, appeared on the tender, boldly flanked 'CAMBRIAN RAILWAYS' in yellow shaded right and below in red. The liberal application of fine red picking round the valences, axle-guards and wheels is not revealed by the blue-sensitive slow plates used by Mr Charles Thomas, who was appointed official photographer to the company in 1899. *Cambrian Official.*

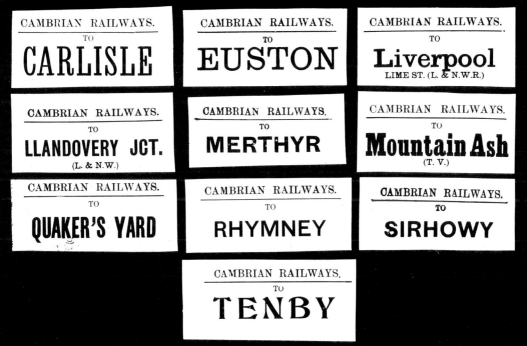

EUSTON STATION. L&N.W.R.

Above: This elegant scene at Euston at the turn of the century shows (extreme left) an Aston tricomposite through carriage. *Raphael Tuck & Sons.*

Left: On 28 July 1900 the old Barmouth over-draw bridge was rolled back for the last time and the Cleveland Bridge and Engineering Company replaced it with the revolving bridge. *Collection C. C. Green.*

Top right: The addition of the Birmingham waterworks to the rota of work for small tank engines was causing problems by leaving only one spare. So No. 22, a standard H type Manning Wardle, Works No. 1523 of 30 June 1901, was bought for £1,100. In 1916 she was sold for war service for £700. At a capital depreciation rate of about £25 per year she must have become one of the most economical workers on record. *Cambrian Official.*

Centre right: At first, Herbert Jones repeated his predecessor's excellent carriage designs, but decked them in resplendent style in keeping with the new engine livery. The gold lining became middle chrome yellow flanked by fine red picking lines; 'CAMBRIAN RAILWAYS' in gold shaded right and below in blue appeared in the top panels, with the feathers as central emblems. The key colours remained bronze-green and white. *Metropolitan RC&W Co Ltd.*

Bottom right: The Tylwch smash, 16 September 1899. Both vehicles were in the restrained Aston livery and re-appeared a few months later in the more showy style. Seen clearly is the gas-piping on top of coach No 266, built by Ashbury's the year before for £1,020. *Courtesy of S. Humphries.*

Below: No 19's chief advance was its single-lever action twin-sliding firebox doors instead of the old oval single-flap type. There was a little 'cheating' in the claim that the engine was Cambrian-built, for Nasmyth Wilson made the boiler and firebox unit and the steam-chest; together with the wheels, these were already all in stock. *Cambrian Official.*

Above: On 31 July 1901 the Oswestry Works turned out No 19, a 4-4-0 generally to the standard Aston-'Large Sharp Stewart' design, and this inspired C. S. Denniss to have a publicity photograph taken of a train built entirely in the company's own works. It was taken at Llanymynech, probably in August, 1902. The six-wheeled passenger brake-vans were No.185 leading and No. 184 at the rear, both completed in 1900. The six first, second and third class (tricomposite) carriages, each with a separate lavatory reached via an internal semi-corridor for each class and having a luggage-locker at the one end, were the latest in comfort and style for through running over other companies' lines. The leading carriage was No 279 and the other five were Nos 278 and 280-283, all newly out of the works in July 1902. The tender was makeshift, as No 19's proper tender did not emerge from the works until 1903. Seemingly C. S. Denniss had grown impatient for his publicity picture and ordered the painting up for the occasion of one borrowed from another engine. Just above the rear of the tender can be seen the girders of the underdeck bridge which carried the Llanfyllin old line across the canal. *Cambrian Official*

Below: The 'Kerry Donkey' just before the three old four-wheeled saddle tanks were replaced by something more modern. A year or so before this picture was taken, a boy of 14 tried to wreck the train by putting an obstruction across the rails. He was sent to prison for six weeks – *with hard labour. Courtesy of R. E Thomas.*

Above: By the water tank at Kerry, It was necessary to edge along the side of the wooden tank to hand the leather 'trunk' over to the filler hole, then hold the valve lever down by hand while the water flowed. *G. M. Perkins.*

Above: The Afon Leri 'Cut' was completed about 1901. This work re-aligned the river to flow directly from Borth to a new exit on the Dovey estuary, thereby draining the marshy area behind Aberleri (now the golf course) and obliterating Borth Harbour and its sea approach. The picture shows Sands Sidings and the cattle pens built for the hoped-for Irish trade before the Leri Cut was made down the opposite foreshore. The schooner is the *Volunteer* (D. Jones, Master) and the tiny gaffsail boats are the ferries operated by father and son John and Edward Bell. *Courtesy of John Burman.*

Centre right: On 4 April 1903, after 39 years of narrow-gauge schemes and counter-proposals, the Cambrian started running passenger services for the 2ft 6in gauge Welshpool & Llanfair Light Railway, using locomotives and stock 'designed' by Herbert Jones in conjunction with Beyer Peacock and R. Y. Pickering & Co. This scene shows *The Countess* on a mixed train at Castle Caereinion in the same year. Her stablemate was *The Earl*. Welshpool & Llanfair stock followed the parent company in its livery and its subsequent alteration. The W&L passenger 'station' was at the edge of the main Welshpool goods yard. *Courtesy of Tom Aldridge.*

Right: Until 1908 all Cambrian goods and passenger brakes had signal red ends. This 13-tonner left the works in December 1902. Two windows and a large removable panel were fitted into the other end. *Cambrian Official.*

Above: In April 1903 R. Stephenson delivered the first of Herbert Jones' 0-6-0 goods engines, the class which took his name as 'The Jones Goods'. Generally they were a very effective design, marred by one major fault which was to show itself fairly frequently, and they lasted in service as well as their predecessors the Aston Goods. Nos 89 to 93 all had good-sized cabs, but the roof was still short of covering the entire footplate. The blemish of the design was that the balance-weights were all in the wrong sectors of the driving wheels; thus the 'Jones Goods' had a disconcerting habit, when running light, of developing a violent rocking motion and hopping off the track at medium speed. Legend has it that one driver dug his trackside allotment on the Saturday, regarded it with satisfaction on the Sunday and cut his bean trenches at 4 ft 8½ in centres with his engine on the Monday. Fortunately most of the mishaps with these engines were only minor ones. *Cambrian Official.*

Centre left: The works could also turn their hand to skilled fine coachwork, as exemplified in this trim-looking parcels van, c 1902. *Cambrian Official.*

Left: The 8-ton crane made by Kitchen of Warrington for Llansaintffraid was re-erected in 1902 at Spion Kop timber yard. Just how many turns of the 'steering wheels' operated by men standing on the platforms level with the carriage waist-line were required to raise the loads is not known. *Cambrian Official.*

Above left: On 5 January 1904 the Cambrian started working the Tanat Valley Light Railway, entirely with Cambrian locomotives and rolling stock, the Sharps 2-4-0 tanks being the usual motive power. Llangynog terminus is seen about 1905, looking down from Rhiwarch Quarry. Berwyn Granite Quarry, formerly the Llangynog Lead Mine, is in the background. *Courtesy of T. Jones.*

Below left: An official inspection party had travelled to Llangynog before the opening in the Directors Saloon (No.9) and the similar No.10, drawn by the contractor's engine – Strachan No.7. *Courtesy of M. E. M. Lloyd.*

Above: Strachan was also giving the local people free trips to the main line in his wagons to help to get them used to the idea of train travel. One lady watched a goods train go by in awe-struck silence and turned to her friend. 'Blodwen!' she cried, 'what a wealthy man that Cam Rys must be to have his name on all those wagons!' Or so an old Cambrian man related. The wagon shown was the company's maid-of-all-work, the 10 ton drop-sided, two-plank slate truck. No 927 was built in Oswestry Works in October 1899 at a cost of £65.50. *Cambrian Oficial.*

Below: Cambrian vans were painted light neutral grey, relieved by black on the outer faces of the external framing. Occasionally the sliding doors jammed through warping, but more often because the load had 'walked' across the floor. The picture is dated 21 March 1904. *Cambrian Official*

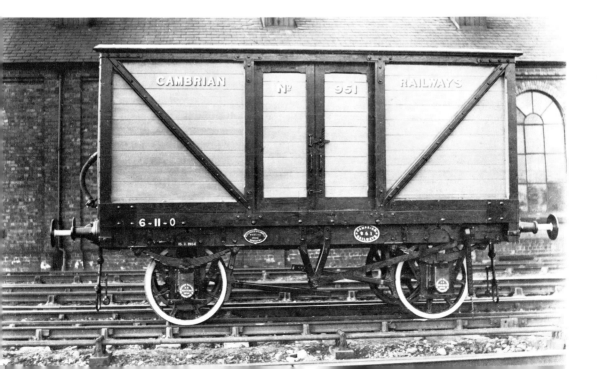

A miscellany of Cambrian-domiciled private owner wagons

Top: Photo dated 1871. *Courtesy of Historical Model Railway Society*

Above left: Photo dated c 1885. *Courtesy of M. E. M. Lloyd.*

Above right: Photo dated c 1897. *Courtesy of Historical Model Railway Society.*

Below: Photo dated c 1910. *Courtesy of C. Meehan.*

Top right: Photo dated c 1910. *Courtesy of M. E. M. Lloyd.*

Centre right: Photo dated c 1920. *Courtesy of J. P. Richards*

Bottom right: Photo dated c 1925. *Courtesy of H. B. Evans.*

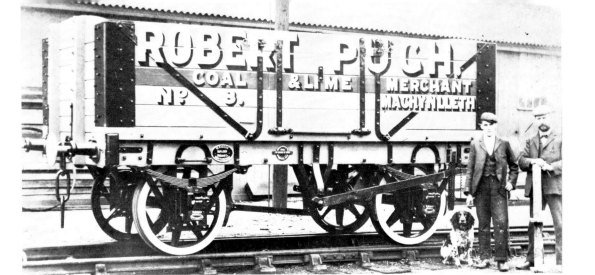

Right: In June 1904 goods trains to Oswestry conveyed the best bargains any railway had from the second-hand market—three efficient tank engines in good order for £2,000 the lot. They went straight into service in their blue Lambourn Valley livery plus cut-out brass number plates. This is Hunslet No 811 of 1903, formerly *Eadweade. Cambrian Official.*

Centre right: Chapman & Furneaux No 1161, formerly *Eahlswith.* The Great Western's quick, low-price sale was inspired by a wish not to take on any engines not of Swindon design – they were then happily in ignorance of what was to come their way in 1922, including a few of their own back. *Aelfred,* a similar engine, became Cambrian No 35. *Cambrian Official*

Below: Also in June 1904 Oswestry Works completed the first two of Herbert Jones' excellent corridor tricomposite carriages. Even the Great Western ran them for nearly 30 years after taking them over. *Cambrian Official*

Far right top: On 11 July 1904 Oswestry turned out their second 'Large Sharps'-type engine, No 11. She had to wait nearly four years for her proper tender. Seen here south of Harlech on the royal staff train on 14 July 1911. *H. W. Burman.*

Below: At the opening of the Birmingham Corporation Water Works on 21 July 1904, King Edward VII and Queen Alexandra travelled in the Directors Saloon and *Calettwr* was fitted with a spark-arrester for the occasion. Shropshire Light Infantry and police guarded the track all the way from Rhayader. The royal train was preceded (officially) from Rhayader by three trains of beautifully dressed officials and VIPs – all sitting in slate-wagons behind engines without spark-arresters. With their finery flying in the wind, two trains' loads got away, if a bit late, but the third's occupants were still sitting loaded as the royal train was due and got shunted. The royal train left 25 min late because it got stuck at the top of the grade and had to have assistance from a Corporation engine as well as from the reserve Sharps, 4-4-0 No 82. So the third train occupants never saw the ceremony and had to be content with the luncheon. That day Rhayader dealt with 91 train movements including one which was kept in orbit between Doldowlod and Builth Wells because there was no unoccupied siding in which to put it. Of the journey in Cambrian slate-trucks Birmingham reporters wrote: 'The trip was thoroughly enjoyed and the spasmodic behaviour of the chain-coupled trucks on each occasion on restarting was productive of much merriment'. *(The Post)* 'A terrible and nerve-shattering trip and the passage of a long tunnel left the bright raiment of the ladies covered with dirt and every throat parched by sulphur fumes'. *(The Chronicle)* 'Trucks packed with mayors, generals, bishops and gaily-dressed ladies started with a jerk which precipitated every one into his neighbour's arms'. *(The Mail)* And of the time keeping – or lack thereof: 'The King was somewhat annoyed by the eccentric hours of the railway company. *'(The Mail)* Even the company's own trainload of bigwigs from Oswestry was late. *Fox-Davies – L & GRP.*

Below: When recording the effects of the head-on 'bump' at Forden on 26 November 1904, the good Mr Thomas dropped the oldest 'clanger' known to photographers. He put his glass-plate into the holder with the emulsion to the back, and reversed his picture. The accident, in foggy weather, was caused by the driver of No 47 over-running signals set at danger because the stationmaster was having horses unloaded from a goods train that was blocking the line, whereas he should have put the goods train into the proper siding. *Cambrian Official*

Above: On the same day that the Cambrian management was having such an anxious time at Rhayader, Stephensons completed No. 94, the first of Herbert Jones' own design of passenger engines. Known as the 94 class, or Stephenson 4-4-0s, they were handsome engines and their performance was good for the difficult line they worked over. Five were built, Nos 94-98, all arriving in 1904. This official photograph of No. 95 was taken at Oswestry late in 1904. *Cambrian Official.*

Top right: Sharps 2-4-0T No 59 about 1905. *Courtesy of R. E. Thomas.*

Centre right: Sharps Goods 0-6-0 No 15 at Llanymynech on the Blodwell Junction train. The tender carries a diminutive spectacle plate to provide some shelter when running to the terminus. Another useful 'evidence' picture – the tender rear panel is still lined. *L&GRP.*

Bottom right: Encouraged perhaps by the success of his second-hand shopping expedition for the Lambourn Valley tanks, Herbert Jones fell for six of Metropolitan Railway's bargain offers. 'Fell' was the operative word, as their high axle-weights and their low coal capacities and hill-climbing performances restricted their use eventually to light local and yard pilot duties. They could just manage to be of some assistance as banking engines up the Talerddig incline. No. 2 was once Metropolitan No 10 *Cerberus.* The other five were Nos 12, ex-11 *Latona;* 33, ex-12 *Cyclops;* 34, ex-13 *Daphne; 36, ex-15 Aurora,* and 37, ex-66 (un-named). *Cambrian Official*

Above: After 1867 the Cambrian had given facilities at Llanidloes and Aberystwyth to the Manchester & Milford Railway. It also exacted payment, which in the case of Llanidloes was truly an exaction – only one train ever got as far as Llangurig, after which the creditors seized the rails and had them sold. In 1906, when the Manchester & Milford's operation between Aberystwyth and Pencader was failing financially, the Cambrian made attempts to get it, but this decrepit line was 'the one that got away', it was leased to the Great Western in that year and Aberystwyth got a foretaste of the future when two 'Dean Goods', numbered 9 and 10 were shedded there. This picture shows M&M No. 10 at Aberystwyth in 1906. *Courtesy of Miss Nichol.*

Below: Llanidloes Station about 1905 – an extremely valuable photograph for modelling detail. Note: a ventilator cover for the full width of the 6ton van in the short carriage-truck bay; the shunt and starter signals to South Yard Neck bracketted on to the warehouse; the point indicator lamps; the small Mid-Wales shed behind the Down Home signal; the Mid-Wales goods brake with 'verandah' at each end; and the liberal use of single-slip diamond crossings. The engines on shed are a 4-4-0 'Large Sharp Stewart' and an 0-6-0 Sharp Stewart Goods. The two ladies in the left foreground are staff of Spiers & Ponds, the refreshment concessionnaires at all principal Cambrian stations. *Courtesy of R. E. Thomas.*

Left: This ingenious mobile test rig for the new water-raising pumps and their driving engine enabled the machines to be moved easily to their permanent building and gives us a close look at an old dumb-buffered timber bolster wagon. The panels on the valve-box ends bear the wording 'MAKERS CAMBRIAN RAILWAYS OSWESTRY WORKS 1906' – such was their pride in their workmanship. *Cambrian Official.*

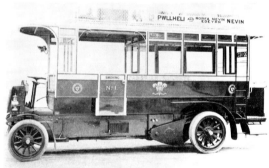

Centre left: While C. S. Denniss tried to get motor-buses for the Cambrian in 1901 he was unable to start a service between Pwllheli and Nevin until two Swiss Orion-chassis vehicles with bodies by Moss & Wood were delivered on 9 June 1906 for £770 each. The two cylinders were horizontally opposed fore and aft, separately water-jacketted and with a huge fly-wheel under the driver's seat. A vee-belt drove a circulating pump in a tank and pipe-coil cooling system visible below the door, and an extremely long, heavy 'silent'-toothed belt drove a massive gear-box to be seen below the feathers emblem. A chain-drive on either side imparted the final drive to the solid back-axle and the wide rear wheel-rims each took two tyres side by side. *Cambrian Official.*

Below: No.22 on a train from the Van mine, about 1905. *Collection C. C. Green.*

Above: Aberystwyth shed. The three even-arm bracket signals were outer homes indicating which route was open towards the platforms and the raised walkway enabled ticket examiners to clear a train before it drew in, with obvious saving in time. The shunt arms again show the pale magenta for danger. *Cambrian Official.*

Left: Between 1906 and 1909 Abraham Williams of Aberdovey rebuilt the wooden trestle section of Barmouth Bridge. Toll charges for using the timber-floored walkway had to be paid *at both ends*, once for entering and once for leaving, ie a lady in a bath chair paid 1d for herself, 1d for the pusher and 1d for the chair four times over if she actually left the toll way at the other end and then returned. *Courtesy of T. I. Hughes.*

Below: In 1907 auto-train working received a brief try-out. Two Sharps 2-4-0 tender engines were rebuilt as tanks and two six-wheeled coaches were cut about and remounted on a bogie-frame to form a trailer. *Cambrian Official.*

Above: Jubilation – the crowd and principal participants in the opening ceremony of the new extension and terminal station at Pwllheli, 19 July 1907. The old main station building was re-built stone by stone at Aberdovey. *The National Library of Wales.*

Below and right: In March 1908 five more 'Jones Goods' were received, this time built by Beyer Peacock & Co. They were curiously numbered 15, 31, 38, 42 and 54, and while No 38 remained unmoved the others were equally curiously re-numbered 99-102 just to boost the Cambrian locomotive numberings into three figures. The Beyer engines had even better cabs than their predecessors; they came right over the footplate on pillars. No 102, the highest number in the Cambrian stock register, is manned by Driver Tom Caffrey on 4 July, 1913. Here is No 101 on Sawmill Siding, Aberdovey. Note the creosote tank for sleepers. *H. W. Burman.*

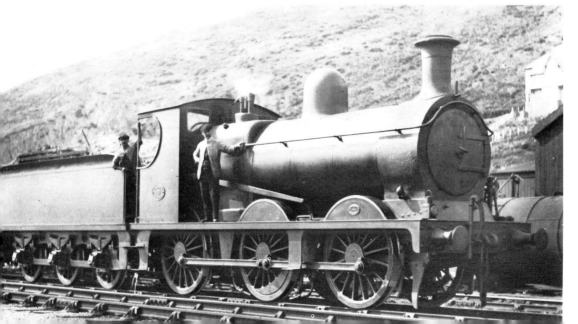

Above: The last pair of Jones corridor coaches were built in 1908 and were locker tricomposites with a diminutive portion at the end for a guard. They were rebuilt as refreshment serveries and became known as the 'Tea Cars'. Many people remember the long struggle down the narrow corridors, climbing over suitcases and squeezing past people to reach and edge their way, elbows tucked in, round the little buffet space – and the perilous return journey. As might have been expected, the buffets were staffed by Spiers & Ponds. *Cambrian Official.*

Above left: Before No 31 had time to be renumbered 100, she shot off the rails on 7 August 1908 in the dip at Nantmawr Junction and towed a horse-box and a Great Central Railways brake-third between the Llanfyllin line and the Ballast Siding, thereby providing the locals with something nearly as exciting to watch as a travelling circus. The driver got the blame and the sack. Maybe the fact that the train was a private charter job moving a director's household goods and farm stock did not help! *Cambrian Official.*

Below left: Dinas Mawddwy, c 1912, with 2-4-0 No 28. *G. M. Perkins.*

Below: In 1908, as part of an economy drive brought about by rising wages, the work in the paintshop was cut by introducing an overall bronze-green carriage livery, relieved by single middle chrome yellow lining. This is Builth Road Station in 1902, with a 2-4-0 on a down train waiting to cross an up train. *G. M. Perkins.*

Above: In 1910 No 21 was the first of the 'Small Sharps' to be re-built with a higher boiler pressure and the shorter Jones chimney; she lost none of her good appearance in the process. She is seen at Aberdovey on 24 September 1912, on the 9.20 up Coast train. *H. W. Burman.*

Below: Afon Wen about 1910. The marked similarity in appearance between the Cambrian rebuilds of the old 2-4-0s and the Webb engines of the London & North Western is exemplified here in Cambrian 2-4-0 No 29 and an unidentified 0-6-2 'Coal Tank'. *Courtesy of Ifor Higgon.*

Top right: On Saturday 29 July 1911, with the aid of a Light Railway Order, a Treasury grant, and a handsome subscription from David (later first Lord) Davies, the MP for Montgomeryshire, the Cambrian re-opened the Mawddwy Railway after an extensive re-construction. Dinas Mawddwy station is here decorated for the occasion. *Courtesy of W. E Hayward.*

Centre right: The completed new Barmouth Bridge, c 1910. *J. Valentine.*

Bottom right: The surviver from the Van Railway at Caersws about 1910. *Courtesy of Evan Howells.*

Right: From 1867 the Cambrian had given connecting passenger and goods facilities adjacent to its station at Cemmes Road to the Mawddwy Railway, until the latter's near physical and financial collapse, which went agonisingly on from 1903 to 1908. In re-opening the Mawddwy, the Cambrian took on yet another old Manning Wardle – by now the oldest, Works No 140 of 1864. Named *Mawddwy*, it was rebuilt before going back into service in 1911 and becoming Cambrian No 30. A similar but heavier workmate, *Disraeli*, was scrapped at the takeover. *L&GRP.*

Centre right: Nevertheless *Disraeli*, via 'her' or 'his' salvaged cylinder block and crank-axle, did good service for many years after the official scrapping date as the works air-compressor. Note the multi-rope drive – a remedy for the 1914-18 wartime shortage of leather? *E. Colclough.*

Below: Decorations for the Royal occasion – Aberystwyth ready for the arrival of King George V and Queen Mary on 15 July 1911, when 'His Majesty the King placed the foundation stone at the north-west angle of the main front of the Great Hall and Her Majesty the Queen placed a corresponding stone on the south-east angle of the same building' – so reads the Report of the Council for The National Library of Wales. *National Library of Wales.*

Far right above: A 'Jones Goods' 0-6-0 arriving at Aberdovey on an up goods in early summer, 1911. *H. W. Burman.*

Far right below: A 'Sharps Goods' 0-6-0 on a southbound local passenger train leaving Harlech, 8 July 1911. *H. W. Burman.*

Above: 'Aston Goods' No 79 on a down Coast goods– two Cambrian vans followed by low two-plank slate wagons – approaching Harlech, 24 July 1911. *H. W. Burman.*

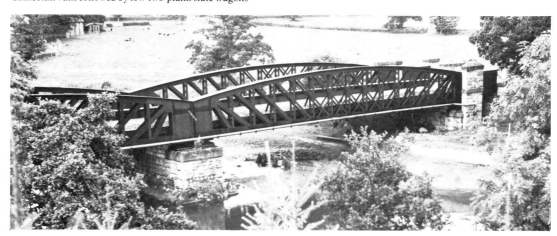

Left: In 1912 the section of line between Newtown and Moat Lane was doubled. The principal feature created through this requirement was the Doughty Bridge across the Severn. *C. C. Green.*

Below Left: Three generations of Stationmasters. Mr Fryer, seen here posed at Abermule with the tablet (marked Abermule and Montgomery, which would authorise the train to go ahead in safety) was the grandfather of the small boy in the photograph on page 22. Later his own son became stationmaster at Abermule. The tablet-controlling instruments were in the low building behind the engine and not in a signalbox. Knowing the Fryers' reputations for the careful working of their stations one can surely say that had the second Mr. Fryer not been on holiday, there would not have been the accident there in 1921, despite the odd arrangement. *Courtesy of W. R. Fryer.*

Above: 'Sharps Goods' No 14 waits at the head of Aberdovey Harbour Branch on 16 July 1912, until the through train signalled on the main line has passed. Note that she is propelling one wagon and will have a short train behind the tender. It was quite normal procedure on the Cambrian to propel or to propel and pull simultaneously in order to work awkwardly placed sidings. *H. W. Burman.*

Below: The extremely popular Vale of Rheidol Light Railway with a gauge of 1 ft 11½ in had been operating from its own terminus near Aberystwyth station since 1902 and had a mixed-gauge exchange siding with the Cambrian near Llanbadarn. It was absorbed into the Cambrian system on 1 August 1913 – the last of a numerous series of takeovers, which brought the total mileage to 241 owned, plus 57 miles worked for subsidiary companies. *Lewis The Mart – A. J. Lewis.*

Above: Much ado about nothing: Sharps 2-4-0 No 53 makes a tremendous pother about taking a turn on the trailer car local on 4 July 1913, leaving Aberdovey. *H. W. Burman.*

Above left: Besides the little Bagnall seen on the previous page (known affectionately by the valley folk as 'Coffee Pot'), the Cambrian took over with the Vale of Rheidol two 2-6-2 tank engines, the only ones ever to have been built by Davies & Metcalfe. As the firm had no experience of designing entire steam locomotives they appealed for help to the Lynton & Barnstaple and received a set of drawings for a narrow-gauge 2-6-2 tank. *W. L. Good.*

Centre left: 'Sharps Goods' No 39 on an up goods appraching Lwyngwril, 9 July 1914. Note the use of lowsided wagons, all two-plank, even for casks as in the one behind the van. *H. W. Burman*

Below left: 'Aston Goods' No 87 approaching Aberdovey station in 1913. The Harbour Branch leading to Sands Sidings and Port Aberdovey is on the right. *H. W. Burman.*

Right: Dignity – The Ticket Inspectors. The summer-relieving inspector at the back wears a uniform hat only. *Courtesy of H. S. Humphries.*

1914 – 1922: The War Years and Finale

The Great War has been de-personalised to mere numbers as the 1914-18 war, and now even further down to World War I to distinguish it from World War II. It was reality to those who lived through it and the four years of neglect it entailed for the Cambrian (and all the other small railways) brought about decline to a point beyond recovery. It revived for the Cambrian very briefly some of the failed mineral workings and created a temporary demand for home-grown timber, mainly for pitprops. But when it was over most of this indigenous freight traffic had gone for all time.

Above left: 'Small Sharps' No 16 near Aberdovey, c 1915. *H. W. Burman.*

Left: There was wartime shortage of engines because several were working the South-to-North 'Jellicoe Specials' on part of the route between the South Wales coalfields and Scapa Flow and others were working out to Shrewsbury, Crewe, and even over to the North Midlands. This prompted the rebuild by Beyer Peacock in 1915 of No 34, one of the ex-Metropolitan 4-4-0 tanks. No 36 was converted at Oswestry in 1916 at less cost. The lighter axle-weight so obtained enabled them to be used more widely, but they were never a success. The tenders came from 'Sharps Goods' 0-6-0s. *Cambrian Official.*

Below left: Despite the war there was still holiday traffic on the coast and 1915 and 1916 saw the conversion of two older six-wheeled coaches into observation cars with reversible tram-type seating, for use on the Coast route. *G. H. W. Clifford.*

Above: 'Large Sharps' No 86 on a north-bound train late one evening in 1915 between Harlech and Pensarn. *H. W. Burman.*

Below: From 1915 onwards, repainted engines appeared in a new livery of broad French grey edged signal red, with the word 'CAMBRIAN' in middle chrome yellow on the tender. 'CAMBRIAN' was also tried out in French grey. The stumpier, built-up Jones chimney replaced the more stylish Aston design. No 79 is at Sands Siding Aberdovey on 12 July 1915. It is not clear whether the change back, not to the old blue-grey but to the 'pinky' French grey, was inspired by a leaning towards the 'Entente Cordiale' with our allies across the Channel, but it would accord with the sentimentality of the time. *H. W. Burman.*

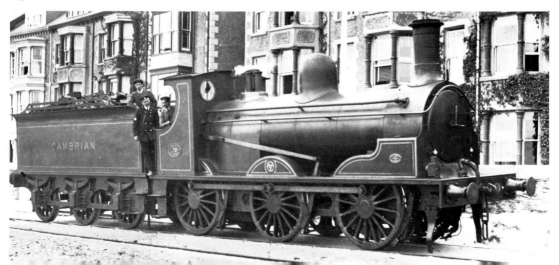

Above: 'Aston Goods' 0-6-0 on passenger duty leaving Aberdovey on 3 August 1918. The train includes one through runner – a GWR coach. *H. W. Burman.*

Left: 'Aston Goods' No 88 leaving Llanbedr for Dyffryn Ardudwy c 1916. *H. W. Burman.*

Above right: No 86 leaving Caersws on a short local train to Whitchurch. The cast-iron notices were painted in white letters on a green background, being the same green (approximating BR parcels road-van green) as was used with white and sometimes a lighter green on the stations. *Collection C. C. Green.*

Right: Barmouth Junction East Box, 1918, with a GWR through train via Dolgelley exchanging tablets. *H. W. Burman.*

Below right: Machynlleth about 1919. 'Large Sharps' No 66 with a Great Western through train via Buttington Junction for Aberystwyth. *H. W. Burman.*

Below: 'Small Sharps' No 50 racing along the estuary wall towards Aberdovey c 1918. *H. W. Burman.*

Right: The Cambrian accomplishes the impossible – two wagons interlocked and both suspended in mid-air. Towyn? *Chief Civil Engineer's Office, NE Region.*

Below: 'Sharps Goods' No 14 entering Machynlleth station in 1919. It is not known whether the running figure wishes to impart some information or wants a lift. *H. W. Burman.*

Bottom: Sharps 2-4-0 No 41 on a Coast local approaching Copper Hill Street Bridge and Craig y Don (No 4) tunnel, Aberdovey, 23 July 1919. *H. W. Burman.*

Left: The period after the Great War was naturally unsettled. Railway revenues could not pay for wages comparable with what the munition workers had been getting and wages restrictions and staff cut-backs led to strikes. So passengers were handling their own luggage in September 1919. Those enormous hats *had* to be worn on the journeys – they simply could not be packed. *A. J. Lewis.*

Below: When the Cambrian trains ceased to run altogether many people 'escaped' from Aberystwyth via the Great Western down the Manchester & Milford route to South Wales. *A. J. Lewis.*

Left: While the original caption to this picture was 'Attempt to stop Great Western Motor Bus at Aberystwyth', the unconcerned manner of the gentleman reading his newspaper with his feet on the mudguard of the bus belies the alleged seriousness of the affair. *A. J. Lewis.*

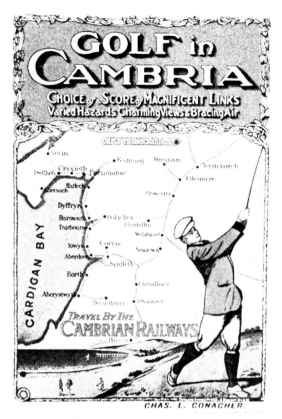

Right and above: Advertising comparisons – Connacher's golfer of 1910 and Williamson's of around 1920 with his bathing belle. *M. E. M. Lloyd and H. R. Thornton.*

CAMBRIA'S CALL TO GOLFERS.

Below: Aberystwyth Station c 1920. In this year on this station at the age of four, the author was spellbound by an engine with big bulgy sloping cylinders, a polished brass dome and an enormous chimney. The following year at Builth Wells, where the boarding house was next to the line, cemented a life-long alliance with dignified shiny black engines with red oval number plates, and the resounding word 'CAMBRIAN' on their tenders. *A. J. Lewis.*

Above: Staff at Aberystwyth about 1920 (strange that a goods train should have been backed right down into a passenger terminus: and one feels that the photographer might have got the wheel-tapper not to hold his hammer as if it was sticking up out of the stationmaster's hat). With the many excursions (including, of course, those to the 1916 National Eisteddfodd), the only carriage liveries these gentlemen are not on record as having seen in their own station were those of the North British and of the Glasgow & South Western. Today's Cambrian modeller is thus free to tell his friends 'Bring your own stock'. *Collection C. C. Green.*

Below: Few photographers caught Cambrian engines 'going foreign', but here is 'Aston Goods' No 74 on a through-running train from South Wales at Merthyr Tydfil. The angle of taking recalls admirably the knack these small engines had of hiding behind their tenders. *H. L. Hopwood: now in Loco Club of Gt. Britain's K. Nunn Collection.*

Above: 'Small Sharps' No 50 on an up Coast train made up entirely of six-wheelers, c 1920. *G. H. W. Clifford.*

Below: 4-4-0 No 36, once the Metropolitan Underground tank engine *Aurora*, at Aberdovey in 1920. *G. H. W. Clifford.*

Above right: One of the last batch of 'Jones Goods' was derailed in Talerddig Cutting, when a landslide (one of many over the years) derailed two engines in 1921. There were no direct services for two days. No 54 is seen on January 19, 1921, the day after the accident. Much worse was to follow. *Edwards Bros. Newtown.*

Right: Abermule, 26 January 1921 – the Cambrian's third 'classic' accident, when the fireman of No 82, a 'Large Sharps', took back from a young porter-signalman the tablet referring to Montgomery – Abermule which he had just traversed. So the train left Abermule heading straight for an express, which had already left Newtown along the single track. After ringing Abermule to see if the express had cleared the section, the station staff at Newtown stood about

in stunned silence. 'We knew what was going to happen; we were waiting to be told where it had happened', they said. *E. Colclough.*

Below right: Abermule, 26 January 1921. Under one coach, four bogies of two different companies. The fireman of No 95 came to his senses walking about down the line from the wreckage and clutching the tablets from both engines. He never recalled the details of his search after instinctively snatching his own tablet before jumping from his engine. The crew of No 82 were both killed, along with the Company Chairman, Lord Herbert Vane-Tempest, and 16 other passengers. The crew of No 95 did go back to driving, but 'kept seeing things coming at them round curves', their mates said. *Edward Bros. Newtown.*

Above: As a hasty stop-gap replacement for Nos 82 and 95, two elderly ex-Great Western engines were bought from the Bute Docks Supply Co. Originally Beyer Peacock 'singles', they had been converted to 2-4-0s. No 10, ex-GW, No 213, is seen at Harlech in 1922. The other was No 1, ex-GWR No 212. *H. W. Burman.*

Below: By contrast with the disaster of January 1921, the Cambrian's association with the greatest influence upon communication and thought the world has ever known slipped by unnoticed. On 15 August 1921 a graceful steam yacht entered the Dovey estuary and was moored at the old quay. The relevent entry in the Cambrian Railways – Port of Aberdovey register reads: *Name and Description of Vessel –*

Yacht *Elettra ; Merchant's Name* – Marconi. The charge was £2.21. That evening the folk of Aberdovey gathered on the quayside wonderstruck to hear organ music broadcast from Waunfawr 40 miles away. Could words and music really climb above Cefn ddu, cross mountains and water, and come steeply down over Fridd cefn isaf to sea level? But by the end of 1922 we had heard '2MT Writtle calling!' Soon after families and friends were gathering each evening around enormous contraptions of valves and coils which served up to six sets of headphones to listen to 2LO London, 5IT Birmingham, and the other early BBC stations. *Photochrom.*

Above: No 77 taking water at Llwngwril in 1921. The diminutive water-tower was at the north end of the up platform; it fed also a water-column at the south end, which was kept from freezing by a built-in coal stove. *H. W. Burman.*

Right: 'Aston Goods' No 78 on a northbound goods train passing the up starter signal of Llwyngwril in 1921. The white disc and the ruby-gold danger glass are still there, but green supplanted white for 'all clear' during the war. *H. W. Burman.*

Below: 'Large Sharps' taking a goods train up the start of the Friog bank from Llwngwril in 1921 – a humbler task than that for which she was designed. *H. W. Burman.*

Above: A Vale of Rheidol train bound for Devils Bridge crossing 'The Black Bridge' in 1921. *W. L. Good.*

Below: Before leaving in 1918 Herbert Jones ordered the Cambrian's last new engines, a further five of his 0-6-0 Goods, from Beyer Peacock & Co, this time all numbered to fill in gaps left from scrappings. Nos 15, 29, 31, 42 and 54 were delivered during 1918 and 1919. No 31 heads an up Coast train south of Harlech in 1921. *H. W. Burman.*

Above right and right: Although the Railways Act 1921, which prescribed the legal and financial framework of the absorption of the small Welsh railway lines into the Great Western system, did not become effective until 1 January 1922, the Great Western took a fatherly interest in their affairs in advance. In the case of the Cambrian the GWR 'lent' them two former broad-gauge 0-4-4 tank engines then running as 4-4-0 tender engines, Nos 3521 and 3546 (seen here at Aberystwyth in 1925), as from August 1921. But useful as she may have been on a short-term basis, No 3521 cannot have been in the best of health when first she steamed over the border; she was back at Swindon for overhaul in 1923. As a loan, these two engines were not a generous one. Actually the book transaction which recorded their transfer noted 'sale'; in the financial climate of 1921 the Great Western gave away nothing. *A. W. Croughton.*

Below right: A valedictory – the management of the Cambrian assembled for a parting photograph on 25 March 1922. G. C. Macdonald (Engineer & Locomotive Superintendent) and S. Williamson (Secretary and General Manager), each dutifully and economically filling two posts, are seated third and fourth from the left. *The Story of the Cambrian.*

From GWR to BR

After 1922 the Great Western took over and for many years the Cambrian system provided the background for the most fascinating period of adaptation and conversion to be found anywhere in railway history. Cambrian engines were modified to such a degree that their own makers would scarcely have recognised them. Many attractive old Western engines were suitable for the work required of them in Wales and survived there, long past their allotted time.

Later all of these were supplanted by the standard types of engine evolved by British Railways. But the character of the line and its needs, although much reduced, remain to this day.

Right: A matter of balance. Old No 93, now Great Western No 892, shows clearly how, by boring four huge holes through the balance-weights on the central wheels and by adding weights in different places on all three pairs of wheels as dictated by tests on the Swindon test-rig, the 'Jones Goods' were made into reliable steady runners for many more years. *G. H. W. Clifford.*

Below: 'Swindon Magic' late on a November afternoon in 1932: No 3259 *Merlin* taking the Pwllheli train out of Barmouth Junction. *Merlin* was built in the 1890s as one of 'Mr Dean's specially designed hill-climbing engines' for use in Devon and Cornwall. *Ifor Higgon.*

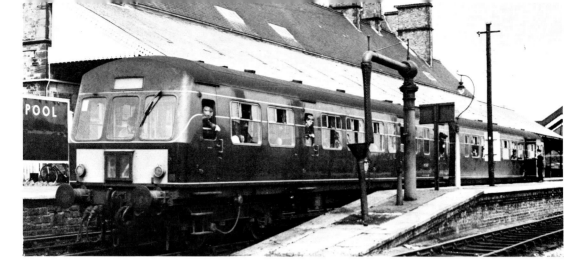

Above: The train had started to move when a passenger raced out of the booking office on the opposite platform and a shout from a porter halted it. Driver, passengers and guard all looked back while the porter shepherded him on board. So the old Cambrian courtesy towards its passengers goes on, reinforcing the Cambrian men's claim that in Wales it was they who took over the Great Western – and latterly – British Rail. *C. C. Green.*

Above left: Swindon through and through? No, just old Mid-Wales No 9 with a boiler and firebox made for a pannier tank, seen here on 27 August 1931 at Barmouth Junction on a goods to Machynlleth – as GWR No 908. The 0-4-2 tank is Great Western No 1155 off the Dolgelley branch. *Ifor Higgon.*

Left: British Railways Standard 2-6-2 tank No 82009 passing Barmouth South Junction on a Pwllheli to Machynlleth local, 15 June 1964. *C. C. Green.*

The Preservation Age

Preservation Groups operating in Wales have, fortunately for the Cambrian, been more in number and in vigour of action than they have been in many other areas. The Cambrian Railways Society has joined forces with the Welsh Railways Action Group, The Cambrian Coast Line Action Group, Transport 2000 (North Wales) and the North Wales Railway Circle in a Joint Working Party for the good of all the Welsh railway services.

Right: The Little Welsh Dragon. Truly the old Great Western has been proved to have been the first and the keenest of all the preservation societies. Their enthusiastic rebuild of all the stock in the 1920s has enabled the Vale of Rheidol line to survive in vigorous working order to this day. British Rail have sponsored The Vale of Rheidol Railway Supporters Association to enable the many people who wish the line well to have a direct interest in its continuing success. *C. C. Green.*

Below: The Welshpool & Llanfair Light Railway Preservation Co. Ltd was incorporated on 4 January 1960. While initially it used the two original engines, *The Earl* and *The Countess*, it very wisely looked elsewhere for more engines and rolling-stock and now runs the finest collection of different 2 ft 6 in or 760 cm gauge trains to be found anywhere. *The Earl* and *The Countess* are seen 'at rest' at Llanfair Caereinion in May 1975. *C. C. Green.*

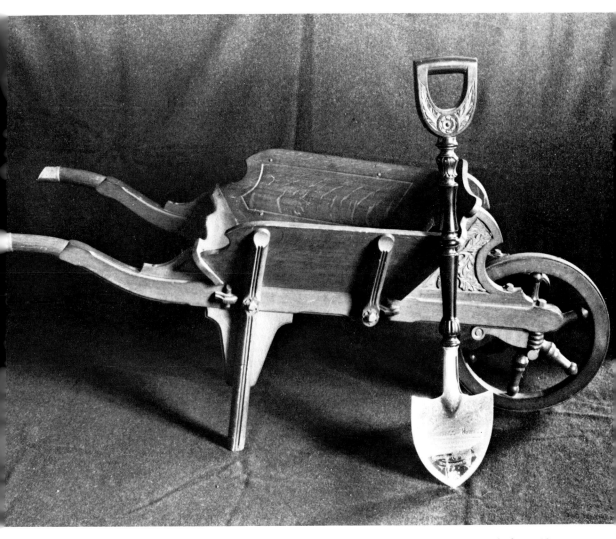

Above: The inaugural celebrations for cutting the first sods on the original little lines have left us with three ornate barrows and five elaborately engraved silver spades. This fine example was presented to The Countess Powis on 12 November 1899 by the Chairman and Board of the Tanat Valley Light Railway and may be seen at Powis Castle. The castle is open to visitors under the auspices of the Powis Trustees and the National Trust. *C. C. Green.*

Above left: Important arrival on Sunday, 12 January 1975. *Foxcote Manor,* which drew the last scheduled train from Oswestry, is housed for the Foxcote Manor Society in the old grain shed leased from British Rail by The Cambrian Railways Society Ltd. as part of their Oswestry operational headquarters. *The Border Counties Advertizer.*

Left: A coach with an interesting career – and a future. No 238 was built in the Metropolitan Carriage & Wagon Co's. works at Saltley in Birmingham in 1895 for £823. Described as a Diagram S, later Diagram 7 tricomposite, she served her passengers well until condemned as Great Western No 6277 on 7 January 1939. During the war she was Wireless Van 40576. Later she became Painter's Coach 80945 and went next to the Wolverhampton Bridge Department as a Mess and Sleeping Van. Now she belongs to Mr. Selwyn Higgins and is at Didcot for restoration. Before transit she was thoroughly vandalised and if anyone knows of the whereabouts of Cambrian axle-box covers, etc. . . . . Seen here at Herbert Road in 1969. *Selwyn Higgins.*

OL-YSGRIF

A dyna'r hen Gambrian. O'i chymharu â chw-mniau eraill, menter fechan ydoedd. Yr oedd prynu dwy injan newydd yn gymaint ymgymeriad iddi ag ydoedd adeiladu deugain i'r London and North Western. Ni fu ei stoc o beiriannau erioed yn fwy na chant, a phrin y cyrhaeddodd y trac dri chan milltir o hyd. Yr oedd llai nag un cerbyd y filltir o drac ar gyfer cario teithwyr a saith wagen y filltir yn unig ar gyfer cludo nwyddau yn lleol yn ogystal ag o fewn cylch ehangach.

Os ydyw ysbryd anturiaeth yn cyfrif o gwbl, yr oedd hon yn fenter fawr, a thrist yw meddwl fod y Ddraig Cymru, Rosyn Coch Lancaster, a phlu Tywysgog Cymru bellach wedi eu dileu.

Postcript

That was the old Cambrian. In comparison with other companies it was a small affair. The buying of two new engines was as large an undertaking as it was for the London & North Western to build 40 or more: and its stock of engines never quite reached the hundred mark. Track mileage barely attained even 300 and its passenger traffic was catered for with less than one carriage per mile of track. Only seven wagons per mile conveyed all its local and outwards goods.

If spirit counts, then it was a great affair. And the painting over of the Dragon of Wales, the Red Rose of Lancaster, and the Prince of Wales' Feathers was something to be regretted.